THE EPIC OF MAN

LIFE

Special Edition for Young Readers

THE
EPIC OF
MAN

BY THE

EDITORS OF LIFE

AND

LINCOLN BARNETT

TEXT ESPECIALLY ADAPTED

BY EUGENE RACHLIS

FROM THE

ORIGINAL VERSION

GOLDEN PRESS  NEW YORK

ACKNOWLEDGMENTS

The publishers are grateful to the Editorial Staff of LIFE and Lincoln Barnett and to the many persons as well as institutions that made *The Epic of Man* possible, both in the version published by Time Incorporated and in this special edition for young readers. Space does not permit a listing of all who have made important contributions of advice and information, but the publishers are especially indebted to Dr. Carleton S. Coon, Curator of Ethnology and Professor of Anthropology, and Robert H. Dyson, Jr., Assistant Curator, of the University of Pennsylvania Museum, for their help and guidance. Specific acknowledgments for the paintings and photographs in this book are made in the Picture Credits on page 172. This list also includes the names of individual copyright owners.

Library of Congress Catalog Card Number: 62-20151

CONTENTS

ACKNOWLEDGMENTS   8

1   MAN'S EARLIEST DAYS   10

2   THE COMING OF RELIGION   22

3   FAMILIES, TRIBES, AND TOWNS   30

4   SUMER: *Reading, Writing, and Arithmetic*   41

5   THE INDUS: *Man Builds Cities*   49

6   EGYPT: *Man Builds a Nation*   57

7   THE MEDITERRANEAN: *Mingling of Nations*   66

8   THE AEGEAN: *Art and War*   75

9   THE ETRUSCANS: *Gay, Gifted People*   85

10   CELTS AND SCYTHIANS: *Wandering Tribes*   95

11   THE SHANG: *Men Who Made China*   109

12   MAYA AND AZTEC: *Men of the New World*   119

13   THE INCA: *Men of the Mountains*   130

14   TODAY'S STONE AGE MEN   140

15   TODAY'S TRIBAL MEN   148

16   THE OLD WAYS GO ON   154

EPILOGUE: FIVE THOUSAND YEARS LATER   165

THE TIMES OF MAN: A CHRONOLOGICAL CHART   170

PICTURE CREDITS   172

INDEX   174

CHAPTER 1

MAN'S EARLIEST DAYS

STEINHEIM MAN

CHANCELADE MAN

ST

NE

NE

NE

HE

CR

CR

NE

CRO-MAGNON MAN

FO
NE

CR

NE

CH

NE

CR

NE

NE

NEANDERTHAL MAN

CHINESE HOMO ERECTUS (SINANTHROPUS)

HE

FONTECHEVADE MAN

HE

NE

NE

AFRICAN HOMO ERECTUS

RH

RHODESIAN MAN

SOLO MAN

SO
HE

FL

FLORISBAD MAN

JAVANESE HOMO ERECTUS (PITHECANTHROPUS)

Of all the creatures on earth, man is the only one who has a feeling that he is something more than an animal. He knows that he is related to other forms of life, and yet he knows something of his own history, too.

Man alone has developed tools and fresh ways to use them; he has painted pictures, shaped clay, wood, and metal; and he has built towns, states, and nations.

On this map of man's world during the Ice Age, the climate conditions are shown in color according to the key at the right. The human figures and letters tell where remains of Ice Age men have been found.

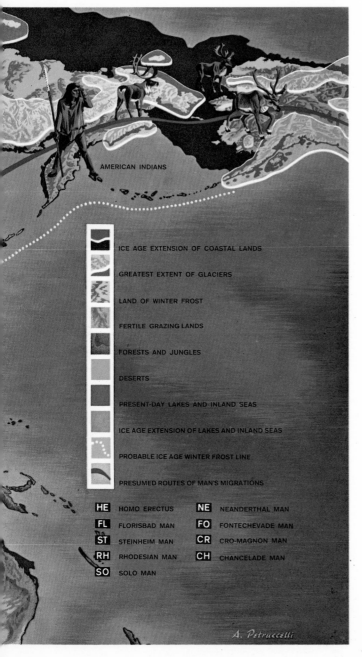

AMERICAN INDIANS

ICE AGE EXTENSION OF COASTAL LANDS

GREATEST EXTENT OF GLACIERS

LAND OF WINTER FROST

FERTILE GRAZING LANDS

FORESTS AND JUNGLES

DESERTS

PRESENT-DAY LAKES AND INLAND SEAS

ICE AGE EXTENSION OF LAKES AND INLAND SEAS

PROBABLE ICE AGE WINTER FROST LINE

PRESUMED ROUTES OF MAN'S MIGRATIONS

HE	HOMO ERECTUS	**NE**	NEANDERTHAL MAN
FL	FLORISBAD MAN	**FO**	FONTECHEVADE MAN
ST	STEINHEIM MAN	**CR**	CRO-MAGNON MAN
RH	RHODESIAN MAN	**CH**	CHANCELADE MAN
SO	SOLO MAN		

A. Petruccelli

The story of these achievements—and man's relationship to other animals—is the subject of a special branch of science we call anthropology. From the discoveries and studies of anthropologists we are today able to trace the epic rise of man from the Old Stone Age to the New Atomic Age.

To understand this story properly we must first place man in animal terms. He is a member of an ancient GROUP of vertebrates—who have internal skeletons. He is of the CLASS of mammals—who have warm blood and suckle their young. He is of the ORDER of primates—who use their fingers and brains. He is of the FAMILY of Hominidae—who walk on their hind legs. He is of the GENUS called *Homo*—man. And finally, he is a member—in fact, the only member—of the SPECIES called *Homo sapiens*, thinking man. *Homo sapiens* has existed for some 250,000 years. Other kinds of men, that is, other members of the genus *Homo*, lived at the time he first appeared, and for many thousands of years before. But thinking man—*Homo sapiens*—is the only one who has remained alive. Today, all men, no matter what their color, size, or ability, belong to this species.

How did this animal we call man happen to last so long and become the most important of all creatures on earth?

We do not know all the answers, although looking for them has become one of the most exciting detective stories in science. The whole history of man's evolution, as we now know it, has been studied in the remains of about two hundred skulls and other collections of bones found in Europe, Asia, and Africa. With so little information to go

Family tree of primates indicates how monkeys, apes, and hominids have been evolving at various periods.

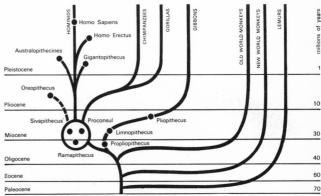

Neanderthal man, seen here hunting the woolly rhinoceros with a stone-tipped spear, endured the Ice Age.

on, anthropologists naturally have had different opinions as to what sets man apart from other animals. But most of them agree that the important physical advantage has been man's erect posture. Other animals before him had walked on their hind legs. Some dinosaurs did, but they did not use their forelimbs, which eventually dwindled into uselessness. Some apes can stand, and even take a few steps. But when they run they must use their hands for support. Only man walks upright at all times. "Man stands alone," an anthropologist has said, "because he alone stands."

With his hands left free to grasp things or to fight, the earliest man found that his way of walking was a great asset. He could seek food and shelter—and thus stay alive—when others could not. As he learned more about what he could do in this posture, the size of his brain increased and he became more intelligent. Soon he thought ahead. Instead of relying on finding sticks and stones when he needed them, he made tools and weapons ahead of time. He became an expert hunter. Some of his tools could cut wood and chip stone, and he carved images. Soon he learned to use language to pass on what he had learned to younger people. And when he found that groups of men fought better or hunted more successfully than individuals, he sought the company of other humans. Out of these groups came new ways of living which

were in turn passed on to other groups. These ways of living, which we call culture, are the bases of human society.

The first primate ancestors of man probably looked like the ring-tailed lemur, which began to climb and live in trees about 70 million years ago. In leaping from one branch to another these first primates developed their fingers and toes. Because they used their fingers to put food in their mouths, they no longer had to seize it with their teeth. As a result, they developed larger jaws and smaller teeth. Some lemurs depended more on sight than on smell, and their vision became more acute than their sense of smell. As they sat up to look at the world their heads became placed vertically on their spines. With improvements, these qualities eventually passed on to man.

There are still gaps in the record from these ancient primates to early man. Scientists generally believe, though, that man and the anthropoid apes are descended from a common ancestor which appeared about 30 million years ago. It is likely that some tree-dwelling primates—descendants of the lemurs—came down to the ground to search for food. Some remained, and eventually walked erect —the hominids which later evolved into man. Others, who returned to the trees, evolved into present-day apes. During this period, some species with a few of the physical traits of man must have lived but eventually disappeared. Remains of some with almost human teeth and skulls have been found in Europe, Asia, and Africa.

Man started his separation from the other animals as his brain became larger. Before *Homo sapiens,* some animals with upright bodies used simple stone tools. They had the brain capacity of modern gorillas, while the first men had brains nearly twice as large. By the time of *Homo sapiens,* brain capacity was not much smaller than it is today. It was the use of the intelligence supplied by this growing brain that allowed man to survive and develop during startling changes in the world around him in the years ahead.

An erupting volcano sends hot lava across the land, and one man, braver than his companions, picks up a burning stick. Thus, the use of fire may have begun.

About 700,000 years ago, just as the genus *Homo* was emerging, the weather of the world underwent a great transformation. For 70 million years or more before that time, most of the world's climate was warm. Then came a gradual cooling, followed by a tremendous movement of ice sheets from the Arctic and mountain peaks. Glaciers of ice thousands of feet thick covered much of the Northern Hemisphere. About 100,000 years later, higher temperatures set in and the ice melted. This was followed by three more similar movements of ice, and at intervals of 100,000 years, other warm periods.

Although we call these glacial periods the Ice Age, there were actually long periods in between of hot weather in many parts of the world. These climatic changes were a strong challenge to early man. He had to learn to live with blizzards and floods, and with freezing cold followed by searing heat. More than anything else, these conditions forced man to move about. As snow and rain froze, ocean levels were lowered. In some places natural land bridges were created. England was connected to the rest of Europe; Australia to New Guinea. Animals moved over these new connections—and man, the hunter, followed them. It is thought that the ancestors of the American Indians crossed one of these land bridges from Asia to Alaska and then wandered south.

Man survived the Ice Age because his brain, growing larger, was able to face the problems of a strenuous, weather-driven existence. Strength alone would not have been enough. Many animals much larger and stronger than man were wiped out during this time. Man adapted to the new hunting grounds of Europe and Asia long before some animals did—and he remained superior when he learned how to use what nature provided.

One of nature's most important gifts to man was fire. Its use, an anthropologist has said, "is the only open-and-shut difference between man and all the other animals." No one really knows when or where man first learned how to use fire. The oldest evidence we have comes from some ancient hearths in northern China. These indicate that some 360,000 years ago, Peking man, a small-brained *Homo erectus*, knew enough to keep himself warm and perhaps even to fashion tools in the flames. But there is no evidence that man could *make* fire that long ago. This important step was not to come for many thousands of years, and even then not to all men.

Before he learned how to make fire, however, man had ways of getting it. Probably the best sources were erupting volcanos or forest fires. At many times and at many places, some man, braver than his fellows, must have picked up a burning brand. When man learned how to handle fire without burning himself, he was on his way to mastering it. He found that dry sticks and leaves would keep fire alive. He could pass this wonderful gift on to others, or carry it with him when he moved to a new shelter. Flaming torches must have passed from group to group, and even from continent to continent.

Fire became the first of man's tools that he did not make with his own muscles. During the last glacial period it permitted him to live in Europe and Asia. It not only warmed him in his cave, but made him a more efficient hunter than he had been. He discovered that animals were deathly afraid of fire. Soon he used lighted torches to stampede the game he sought. And then, one incredible day, he found that the meat of the animal was easier to eat after it had been in the fire.

With the discovery of cooking, which breaks down the tough fibers of meat, man's lot improved. Although his jaws were tough and his teeth fairly large, eating had taken a good deal of his time. His life, in fact, was probably one continuous round of hunting and eating. Once he began to cook, he could eat all he needed in a few hours. The rest of the day could be used for hunting, tool-making, and other activities.

The ability of man to make tools for his future needs is another of the unique differences between him and other animals. He has gone from crude axes and spears to machines which carry him into outer space, move him at incredible speeds, and make thousands of jobs easier to perform. But for nine-tenths of man's existence his only tools were chipped stones or simple shafts of wood.

An Aborigine of northern Australia carries a wallaby, or small kangaroo, the result of a day's hunt. Like Stone Age man, the Aborigine lives by hunting game.

Old Stone Age man is depicted here in some of the stages through which he may have passed. The setting is one of the many open rock shelters, or mouths of caves, where men lived while ice covered much of Europe.

At far left, a stone hammer and wooden punch are used to strike sharp flint blades. Later came spear points made from antlers (left foreground), and eventually straight-backed knives to skin reindeer (above).

In the oldest stage of man's culture—at the beginning of what we now call the Old Stone Age —man made two kinds of tools. Core tools, such as hand axes, were made by pounding a core of hard flint until it had a sharp point. Flake tools, usually scrapers and cutters, were made from the chips—or flakes—which came off the flint during the pounding. From about 300,000 to 100,000 B.C. the flaking process improved as man found more uses for the flakes. He attached them to wood or bone handles to form crude spears. Sometime between 100,000 and 35,000 B.C. sharp points were put on longer handles for better hunting or used separately as scrapers to make skins into clothing to wear against the glacial cold.

Clothed for the weather, the men who remained in the north developed more useful tools. The invention of the flint blade (about 35,000–28,000 B.C.) made the leather thong possible. This led to improved dressing of animal skins and the lacing of them for better clothes. Later came the burin, a chisel-like tool which could split and shape materials that were softer than stone. The burin in turn made possible a whole new series of tools made from animal bones and horn. In time came a straight-backed knife, finer flaked points, and, by the end of the Old Stone Age (8000 B.C.), needles with eyes, barbed spearheads, and even a kind of saw.

The improvements in tool-making made later generations of man a more powerful hunter than his ancestors. With his new tools, man found he need not fear even the mighty mammoth, the largest land-dwelling animal he had to face. His long spear, fire, and his intelligence made him mightier than any animal.

These discoveries were followed by one even more remarkable: A group of men working together were better hunters than the same number working as individuals. Communities were formed for cooperative hunts. They organized attacks on herds of wild horses or other animals which single

In final stages of the Old Stone Age, man learned to produce flakes by pressure (left), which gave him thin, leaf-shaped blades from which he made fine points for weapons. The bone needle, used by the woman on right, led to handsome leather clothes.

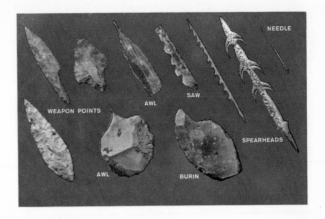

These tools and weapons of late Stone Age man give some clue as to how he survived the years of ice.

hunters could never have made. In France, the bones of 100,000 wild horses have been found in one spot. In Russia, the bones of mammoths have been uncovered at the bottom of what were probably man-made pits. Organized hunting means that there must have been teamwork and leadership—the first steps toward some kind of government.

Man also learned that his new tools could bring pleasure beyond their usefulness in the hunt. With them, he started to carve the images of animals, birds, fish, and insects. Most of those shown on these pages were cut from the antlers of reindeer, and were sometimes used as spear throwers. They indicate that even as man moved toward group activity, there was room for individual expression. Both were to become more highly developed and to take on fresh importance in the years to come.

A bison carving from the late Stone Age shows the head twisted back to fit the shape of an antler.

A stampede of wild horses is started by late Stone Age men in a European valley. Driving the horses up a slope to a cliff, the hunters keep them in line with bonfires and torches. The terrified animals are driven to the edge of a precipice where they are forced to leap to their death. At the bottom of the cliff other members

of the hunting party finish off the wounded horses and begin to carve up the dead for food and skins.
The wild horses of this glacial period were small, stocky creatures with shaggy hair and powerful jaws.
Evidence of systematic hunts for these animals and others implies teamwork, an important social advance.

CHAPTER 2

THE COMING OF RELIGION

On the morning of September 12, 1940, five teen-age French boys were on a rabbit hunt in the woods near their little town of Lascaux. Suddenly their dog Robot vanished. The boys raced to the spot where he had been and found a hole in the ground left by an uprooted tree. With knives and sticks they enlarged the hole until they could

This talisman, a hunting symbol of the Stone Age, was found in the Dordogne area of southern France.

squeeze into it. One by one they entered, and found themselves sliding down twenty-five feet to the floor of an enormous room. They struck matches, which gave them enough light to find Robot. In the flickering glare they also saw that on the walls around them were drawn the outlines of giant-sized bulls.

The boys crawled out of the cave and told the townspeople of their discovery. In a few days, Lascaux was visited by Abbé Henri Breuil, a French priest who is the world's leading authority on cave art. He was overwhelmed by the quality and quantity of the paintings in the cave at Lascaux. The loss of a hunting dog had led to one of the greatest stores of information about early man's gropings toward religion.

The cave at Lascaux is one of about a hundred which so far have been found decorated with paintings, etchings, or carvings from the Old Stone Age. New ones are being opened each year. Some caves have contained examples of early man's art which could be carried from place to place—small statues, carvings, and painted stone and metal. Still others have revealed graves which were carefully prepared and decorated. These discoveries have helped us understand the part religion and magic played in the life of early man. They reveal how he may have felt about the mysteries of life and death and of the wonders of nature.

Lively animal portraits are created on cave walls by skilled Stone Age artists about year 10,000 B.C.

Four Stone Age boys are led to the ceremony which marks their entrance into manhood. They have been tested for courage, and instructed on their adult duties. The shaman, or high priest (right), welcomes them in reindeer dress.

24

The story that the caves in France, Spain, Germany, and Italy tell is of early man trying to reach beyond his own immediate world. He saw the sun rise and set and the moon and stars appear, but could not imagine what caused these great events. Earthquakes, floods, and lightning threatened his life in ways he could not overcome. Death itself was the biggest mystery of all. Under the harsh conditions of the Old Stone Age, most people died young; scientists believe that less than ten percent lived to the age of forty, and only one percent reached fifty.

It probably seemed to primitive man that the only possible explanation for these awesome and fearful occurrences was that they were controlled by some unseen power. It was natural, therefore, to honor this power so that it would look with favor upon him.

In most of the caves in which pictures and carvings have been found there have been no traces of tools or animal bones. This has led scientists to conclude that the caves were held sacred and were used only for special rites. In these ceremonies, the wall paintings and little statuettes played an important role. Some of the paintings show bleeding wounds in animals; others have holes made by actual spears. In these ways early man may have convinced himself that he had won a mystic power over the animal's spirit, and so would be successful

Stone Age statuettes like these suggest that some early men may have worshiped a "mother goddess."

A funeral ceremony as it may have been conducted in France 10,000 to 14,000 years ago is depicted here. In the

in hunting him. Paintings of man himself are very rare, and when they appear they are usually unrealistic or are covered by masks. This may have been because man feared he would be a victim of his own magic.

The pictures themselves, many of them very beautiful, were outlined in the stone walls and ceilings with the use of the burin. The outlines were then filled in with natural pigments of red, yellow, black, and brown. The colors were mixed

center, a mourner places reindeer antlers on a burial mound while the shaman, in bison dress, holds a bison horn.

from mineral oxides and charcoal, and held together by animal fat. Sometimes they were molded into a kind of crayon or, more often, were blown onto the stone through bone tubes. The limestone gradually absorbed the colors, and the darkness and constant humidity of the caves have kept them fresh through the years.

Many of the paintings are impressive as fine art, aside from their value as a guide to the life of early man. At Lascaux, an enormous fresco of finely

drawn bulls includes one that measures seventeen feet in length. The details are skillfully worked out in each animal, whether a horse, cow, bull, or reindeer. The variety has amazed students of cave art, but one painting at Lascaux is the most puzzling of all. It is of an animal with the body of a rhinoceros and the head of a Tibetan antelope. Another, of a wounded bison glaring at a dead or dying hunter, is one of the few which shows a human figure. In some caves, animals are depicted with arrows and boomerangs flying around them.

The ceremonies held beneath the paintings are thought to have been of two main kinds. Those known as "rites of passage" were held to celebrate important changes in the lives of individuals—marriage, death, boys entering into manhood. Those that we call "rites of intensification" dealt with crises affecting the whole group—famines, storms, epidemics. Both kinds were usually conducted by a leader who was supposed to talk directly to the spirits and pass their messages and wishes on to the group. Anthropologists call this leader a "shaman."

Boys were instructed in their adult duties by the shaman. When he felt that they understood these duties and had shown courage in the face of physical loss—often the amputation of a finger—he prepared their initiation ceremony. These were solemn but also joyous events, perhaps the most important in the life of Old Stone Age man.

Death called for another kind of ritual. There is evidence that the dead were given special treatment as many as 80,000 years ago. Bodies have been found buried in an attitude resembling sleep, and graves covered with thin layers of charcoal as though fires were lit to warm the dead. For protection against animals, burial places were often walled with slabs of rock. At the funeral ceremonies, the shaman placated evil spirits while the family of the dead gathered to properly prepare the body. Often a corpse was tied, perhaps to keep its spirit from bringing harm to the living. Food, jewelry, and weapons were frequently left with the body, probably to help the dead person get along in his new existence.

Stonhenge sanctuary on Salisbury Plain, in England, is a monument to religious feelings of early man.

Hunting ceremonies were held to insure a continuing supply of animals and to maintain early man's supremacy over them. One ritual involved the cave bear, whose bones have been found carefully preserved and arranged on slabs of rocks. An anthropologist has called them "the oldest altars of sacrifice so far known." These rites appear to have started when man discovered that the cave bear was easy to kill. The animals weighed as much as a thousand pounds and had very long teeth and claws, but they were awkward and slow moving. They became an important source of food and clothing. Because the cave bear was such a useful animal, it is probable that the special rites were held to try to keep him from disappearing.

Toward the end of the Old Stone Age, as the glaciers pulled back from Europe, the climate grew considerably warmer and man started to come out of the caves. His old art and shrines were left behind, so he created new ones for the ceremonies which were now carried on outdoors. For several thousands of years, man's religious rites were conducted in tremendous open-air enclosures formed by large pillars and slabs of rocks. Scientists have named them megaliths, which means great stones. The most famous megalithic center today is Stonehenge, in England. Others have been found in Scandinavia, Ireland, France, Portugal, Spain, Italy, and Malta. One sacred enclosure, in the Brittany province of France, is two and a half miles long, and is made up of 2,935 upright stones called menhirs.

Scholars are uncertain about the forms of the rites held within the megaliths. If there ever were paintings or carvings, which might have given us some of the clues we have found in caves, they have been destroyed by time and nature. But the stones themselves tell a good deal, and there is general agreement that the megalithic religion was mainly involved with two things: death and the sun.

The concern with death, or the grave, is indicated by the basic form of the megalith architecture. Two upright stones topped by a slab appear over and over again. This not only resembles a tomb, but some of the monuments were actually used as tombs. The tremendous size of some of the forms has led to the theory that they were used for the worship of the dead—perhaps ancestors who were beginning to be thought of as gods.

The megalithic concern with the sun is shown by the arrangements of the slabs. In many cases rows of them are lined up with the path of the sun. At Stonehenge, a great stone arch near the central altar frames the setting sun at the exact moment of its winter solstice. According to ancient myth, this is the moment that the sun god dies and is reborn. Other objects from this period lend support to the theory that the sun was important in early man's religious feelings.

It is as if, after a long stay in gloomy caves, man was joyously lifting his eyes toward the source of the earth's light.

Temple doorway at Mnajdra, on the island of Malta, stands flanked by two large upright "altar" stones.

CHAPTER 3

FAMILIES, TRIBES, AND TOWNS

The last retreat of the glaciers, which started about 20,000 years ago and is still going on, was the beginning of the end of the Old Stone Age. Trees and plants took root, lakes and rivers were formed by the melting ice, and man moved from caves to the outdoors. By 8000 B.C. a new period —which scientists call the Mesolithic or Middle Stone Age—was about to begin in man's development. At different times in different places this gradually became the Neolithic or New Stone Age, the last period of man's preparation for what we term civilization.

The preparation was gradual, but even so, progress was made much more rapidly than in the Old Stone Age. The change from the cave to the open, from suffering in cold weather to enjoying the warm, had a profound effect on man's activity. As he spread out across the land, living in forest clearings and near water, his methods of gathering food changed greatly. The largest animals had been killed off by now or had traveled north with the ice and died there. But other creatures on land and in the water were plentiful, and man worked out new ways to capture them.

There is even evidence that newly invented tools and weapons were made in a kind of factory. At Star Carr, in Yorkshire, England, anthropologists have uncovered a stage 230 yards square. It stood by the shore of a now vanished lake. On a platform built of birch and brush piled in layers on stone and clay, Mesolithic craftsmen worked with deer

antlers and moose antlers. They fashioned spear points, daggers, scrapers, and their new inventions —mattocks, microliths, and probably bows and arrows.

The mattock looks something like a pickax with one end broadened. Its blade was made from antlers and a hole was provided for a wooden handle. With the mattock, man was able to dig through tangled roots for edible bulbs, to cut trees and shape wood. Soon he shaped coracles—circular tublike boats—dugout canoes, and rafts to travel on water. To haul heavy loads on land, he devised sleds, and for his own winter travel, skis.

Microliths are small triangular pieces of flint which were used as barbs on arrows and spears. These permitted man to hunt the smaller animals and fish which were now available. No one knows for sure exactly when and where bows and arrows were invented, but they were in common use in Mesolithic times. Until the rifle was perfected 9,000 years later, they were man's most efficient hand weapons.

The stage at Star Carr indicates that men were gathering in communities at about this time. The first groups were probably blood relatives held together by a single leader. They very likely lived in deerskin tents near a good food supply, and

Learning to gather fish as a source of food was one of man's early achievements. Here, primitive Danes are depicted emptying salmon from their fish trap.

shared food and tools for the benefit of the whole community.

Working together regularly these early groups became superb hunters and fishermen. They started to study the migration habits of fish, and discovered that they were always available, which was not true of land animals. They invented new ways to catch fish—with hooks, nets, traps, and three-pronged spears. And when fish were caught in quantity man learned to dry and store them for future use.

The change from Mesolithic to Neolithic came when men began to cultivate the soil and to keep tame animals. There is reason to believe that farming started between 6000 and 7000 B.C. somewhere in the low, sunny hills that run from Asia Minor eastward through northern Iraq and Iran toward southern Asia. By 3000 B.C., farming was practiced in Europe, and not much later in America and the rice fields of Asia.

The actual ways in which Neolithic men and women started to farm are not known. The best guesses are that in a warm, dry climate, broken by rainfall, they found wild wheat and barley and wild versions of sheep, goats, cattle, and pigs. Women were probably the pioneers in gathering fruits, nuts, roots, and seeds to fill out daily diets. In the Old Stone Age they had already learned to remove the hulls and soften the kernels of wild cereals. They may have learned to use their sharp tools to cut away useless plants which interfered with the growth of grains.

The tools shown below were fashioned by Mesolithic craftsmen from water-softened deer and moose antlers.

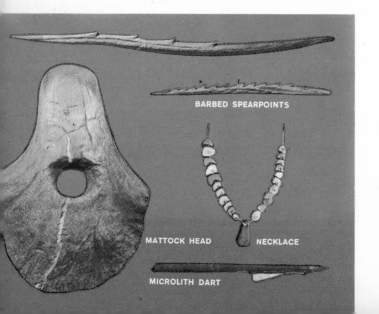

BARBED SPEARPOINTS

MATTOCK HEAD   NECKLACE

MICROLITH DART

Neolithic women may then have found that when seeds were thrown into discarded garbage, which acted as a fertilizer, luxuriant growths often followed. From this may have come early experiments in putting seeds in the soil. Rough fields of grain, probably overrun with weeds and wildflowers, spread over the Middle East. Animals came to these fields foraging for food. Perhaps some farmers brought home baby lambs or goats as pets. The women protected the animals until they were grown. In time, flocks were raised.

It is still a mystery, though, how the bigger and stronger animals — cattle, camels, and horses — were brought under man's control. One theory is that they grew fat on the grain and husks they found in the early meadows, and soon became completely dependent on man's farming. Another is that hunters captured young animals and drove them to rock-enclosed valleys from which they could not escape. Whichever theory is most true, Neolithic farmers had a constant supply of meat without the risks of hunting. By selective breeding, the wild cow eventually became a source of milk and cheese, and domestic sheep and goats gave better fur than their wild ancestors.

The farming skills spread quickly. One of the most famous of the early farm lands is called the Fertile Crescent. This is a large area running north from Egypt through Palestine and Syria, and turning south through the valley of the Tigris and Euphrates Rivers. Today it is mostly desert, but in Neolithic times it was fertile and productive. There, man may have started his first fruit orchards of dates, figs, and olives. He may have made his first wine from grapes and his first beer from grain. Most importantly, he may have learned to breed plants and seeds for hardier and better varieties. At the northern parts of the Fertile Crescent a wild, small-kerneled wheat with a thick hull and a spiky "beard" called emmer was probably grown. This was developed into the types of grain which still give us white flour and bread.

Farming and stock raising brought Neolithic man to a major change in his whole way of life.

By 7500 B.C. man's tools had vastly improved. Here, a man is seen attaching flint barbs to spears with pitch which he gets from heated rolls of birch bark.

In the background above, two hunters, one wearing his antler camouflage and holding a bow, return from the hunt with a slain deer and a captured fawn. At the far right workmen look up from their task of making

spearheads out of water-softened antlers. In the foreground, center, a woman and a man unload more antlers from a skin-covered coracle. Efficient tools enabled Mesolithic man to fashion this watercraft.

He had to stay in one place to manage his new activities. From this need grew the early villages, which were simply clusters of houses within walking distance of the fields and pastures. Villages varied according to their locale. In open areas like Mesopotamia, the first houses were made from mud, which hardened in the sun, and were covered with loose branches and clay. In the forest areas of Europe, houses were built around frames of wooden poles which were covered with sticks and clay. The roofs were usually peaked to shed rain and snow. In Russia and central Asia, houses were made of earth and woven grass.

As villagers and farmers, men and women lived longer than they did as hunters. Those over forty performed some of the easier tasks, such as milking and weaving. Children, who in the Old Stone Age could do nothing until they were old enough to hunt, now tended animals or did light farming chores. Women milled grain, baked bread, and started to fashion pottery from clay. Because farmers are always concerned with the weather, rain priests and wind priests took the place of the old hunting shamans. Each village probably had its own local spirit or god who was believed to guard the people who lived there.

As far as we can tell, dwellers in one village not only worked with each other, but with those from other villages as well. The first steps in trading probably were made at this time. A village with extra wheat, for example, would exchange it with one that had extra building clay. Some of these villages seem to have survived for centuries without suffering the destruction of war.

As villages and populations increased, Neolithic man started to look for fresh land to farm. By the late Neolithic period he started to live and work on the plains by the Tigris and Euphrates Rivers. There the soil was wonderfully fertile from being built up by river deposits. But the area also presented many problems. Some of the land was so dry that nothing could grow on it unless water was regularly fed to it. Some was so wet it could not be used unless water was drained from it. At

Decoration on vase is an early landscape painting

times the two rivers flooded the surrounding countryside; at other times there was scorching heat and drought.

The solutions to these problems were feats of man's courage and intelligence. To protect his fields, he worked out simple systems of flood control. The silt which the rivers left on their banks each year was built up with other soil. These became dikes, or levees, which kept the flood waters from returning to the rivers. During a dry spell, holes were punched in the dikes, and ditches were dug to lead the water to the dusty fields. These projects were such large undertakings that they led to a more complicated group system than the village. Many people were now needed to perform many kinds of tasks. In this area of the world, the town came into existence.

Larger communities brought a new burst of creative energy. Neolithic man invented the plow, and farming was done more efficiently than ever. He trained cattle to pull the plows, and built sledges to hold his farm products. He probably invented the sailboat, too, and the rivers became broad highways. This spurt in transportation led to commerce and trade. Soon farmers and herdsmen from one town visited those at another town on the banks of the Euphrates and Tigris. They exchanged goods with each other, and were visited by townspeople from Persia, Egypt, and the Red Sea. They gave their farm goods for crude jewelry the strangers brought.

Flight of geese is an easy target for these bowmen in a northern European marsh. Some arrows are tipped with flint; others have wooden heads to stun birds.

37

The kernels of barley above, enlarged in this photograph, are upwards of 8,000 years old. Small branch of grain at left suggests it was cultivated barley.

Equipped with sickles, farmers of the New Stone Age (at right) glean wheat and barley in Mesopotamia. In the background stand the mud huts of their village.

Recent discoveries show that the towns were well built. In one of them, houses were made of walls three feet thick, had windows, double doors, and sometimes a second story which was reached by a stone staircase. One building was a potter's workshop where beautifully painted jars and bowls were made. Housewives wore the jewelry which their husbands took in trade. Men played a game something like jacks in which they used the knucklebones of cattle. In another town, a strong wall and a twenty-five-foot-thick tower protected the residents.

In his houses and behind such walls, late Neolithic man could work and develop in security. Soon, with improved transportation, he would begin to extend his interests. He was ready to end what we call the prehistory of man, the long span of time for which we have no written records. He had finished the foundations for the history that was yet to be made.

The clay sickle below was one of the implements used by Neolithic farmers. The farmers on the next page are using sickles that are made of blades of flint.

The ridging in the pottery tray below was designed to remove the husks from grain. Pottery containers made it possible for Neolithic man to store grain.

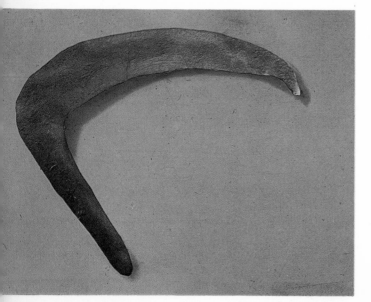

CHAPTER 4

SUMER
Reading, Writing, and Arithmetic

One day, more than 4,000 years ago, a schoolboy in a city not far from the Persian Gulf made some notes in a diary. "I recited my tablet," he scratched in clay, "ate my lunch, prepared my [new] tablet, wrote it, finished it." Either he did not do his lesson properly, or he was naughty that day, for the unknown boy was flogged by his teacher. In desperation, the boy asked his father to invite the teacher home for a meal. The father not only did this, but also provided the teacher with "a new garment" and a "ring on his hand." Not long after that, the teacher announced that the boy had "become a man of learning" and would one day "reach the pinnacle of the scribal art."

The American archaeologist who uncovered the pieces of clay which tell this story calls it "the first case of 'apple-polishing'" in history. It took place in one of the cities of Sumer, which were built along the banks of the Tigris and Euphrates Rivers. Although it is amusing to find that schoolboys that long ago had their problems—and ways of solving them—the tablets of Sumer have a more important story to tell us. These cities—which the

Old Testament calls "land of Shinar"—were where man invented the wheel, first learned to read and write, and to use numbers, money, and metal.

Between 4500 and 2900 B.C. man gradually moved from a simple to a more complicated way of living. For the next five hundred years this new way of life was centered in the cities of Sumer in the Fertile Crescent. These cities were constructed

Memorial statue (right) of Dudu the Scribe who lived around 2500 B.C. in Lagash, a Sumerian city-state.

Military chariot at left bears a wounded soldier to the gates of a Sumerian city. The yoked animals are onagers, Asiatic wild asses tamed by the Sumerians.

In the temple workshops pictured on these two pages, Sumerian craftsmen perform their tasks. At left, above, a workman carries a bundle of finished spears. There are three metalworkers seated behind him. One is removing bronze spearheads from a clay mold, the second is opening a mold to remove a bronze axhead, and the third is working a design on a silver vessel. The men in the group in the center are transacting a

sale of copper and silver ingots. A temple aide holds the balance; another adds stone weights to the weighing pan at left while a young trader places silver ingots in the pan on the right. Above them an older trader discusses the deal with a bald-headed temple administrator. A bearded scribe is taking notes. The workshops above, and others not pictured, surrounded the courtyard of the Temple Oval at Khafajah.

A dinner party in a Sumerian home about 4,500 years ago is serenaded by a harpist (left) as guests eat and drink.

outside walled areas that protected high temples. The temples, called ziggurats, rising above the flat plains, became the centers of Sumerian life. Some scholars believe they were built so tall because the Sumerians felt gods had to be worshiped from "high places."

The Sumerians put a great deal of faith in their gods. They believed that man was created to serve the gods and was always dependent on them. Sometimes the gods were kind, sometimes cruel. Either way, the Sumerians felt man was helpless to do anything about it. One of the poems they have left behind contains these lines: "Mere man—his days are numbered, whatever he may do, he is but wind."

The Sumerian gods were given human forms and faces when they were made into statues. Some gods were universal; others controlled only a single city. High priests and rulers were their earthly servants, but had power only as long as the gods gave it to them. The four most important gods in Sumer represented forces of nature. Anu was the god of the all-encircling sky. He was the foremost among the gods. Beside him stood Enlil, god of the storm, who carried out the wishes of the gods. Third in line was Ki, or Nintu, a goddess who stood for earth or birth. With her was Enki, god of growing things and life-giving waters.

The statues of these gods and many others stood in the temples, which were considered their homes. The high priest who ruled on their behalf lived in rooms adjoining those containing the statues. The gods were believed to own the cities and all the people in them, and many of the fields beyond the walls. These were tilled in the name of the gods, and the harvest was carried to the temple. Because the gods were thought of as humans, priests brought them food and wine three times a day.

44

The Sumerian city's entire life revolved around the temple. Within the building itself were workshops for bakers, brewers, weavers, smiths, and clerks. In another group of rooms craftsmen worked stone, metal, and clay, and businessmen carried on their trades. Here, the Sumerians developed skills which were to be crucial to mankind. Before the cities of Sumer, man had already learned that metals could be melted out of ore, and hammered or cast into useful shapes. Then he made another important discovery: that tin and copper together made bronze, which was harder and tougher than either metal alone. The Sumerians perfected their methods of metal making and it became their biggest business.

Because they needed ores to make bronze, trading over long distances became necessary. The Sumerians imported metal, wood, and stones from foreign places, and exported finished products. These included textiles, jewelry, and weapons which were made by men who became specialists in certain items. As trade increased, new methods were needed to make it work smoothly, and the forerunner of arithmetic was invented. Before 3000 B.C., Sumerian accountants used number systems based on tens and on sixties. The first has given us our decimal system. The second led to our way of telling time and of dividing circles into 360 degrees.

Although this knowledge started in the temples, its use went beyond them. Soon, Sumerians were using weights and scales, and knew how to measure volume, length, and area. As the traders traveled to places as far away as Egypt, India, and Anatolia, they carried this new knowledge with them. The Sumerians used barley, copper, silver, and gold as we use money. Coined money did not come along until much later, but the Sumerians gave a value to the weight of these things and thereby developed the *idea* of money.

To make the system really work required one more invention. This invention was writing—the greatest gift left by the Sumerians. Around 3500 B.C. ancient scribes were still using sharp reeds to scratch pictures of human heads, fish, trees, and spears onto rough tablets. Over the years —possibly a thousand—these pictures began to stand for syllables instead of things. The pictures

Sumerian tablets carry man's earliest known writing.

themselves slowly changed to wedge-shaped marks —which we call cuneiform writing—that were pressed into clay. Later, the Assyrians, Babylonians, and Persians copied this system from the Sumerians. The Egyptians used a different system, but it also comes from Sumer.

The Sumerians used their writing for more than business dealings. As a result we have many hymns, poems, and accounts of their daily life—from a schoolboy's problem with a teacher to the passing of new laws. The Sumerians lived under many laws, some of which we would recognize today. They had a city council, and courts to hear grievances. Some laws were quite strange. Some of the strangest pertained to slaves who were captured in the course of battle. Slaves could own land, do business, and buy their freedom. They could even file a complaint if they were being sold to an owner they did not like. But the laws also permitted their owners to brand or flog slaves, and they were often mistreated. Another law allowed a man to sell his wife and children into slavery for three years in order to pay his debts.

Clay model is exact replica of a Sumerian sailboat.

Archaeologists agree that the slaves were the lowest class in Sumerian life. But beyond this, there is a difference of opinion. One scientist believes the Sumerian records show that "all members of the community were equal." Another feels this was not always true, that the priests, government officials, and soldiers were in an upper class. Below them came the merchants, teachers, laborers, farmers, and craftsmen, followed by the slaves.

Whichever theory is true, the Sumerians for the most part lived very well. They used furniture in their homes which were made of sun-dried brick. They ate well, too. Salmon, roast pig or lamb, fruit, goat cheese, beer, and wine were served at meals. Dinner guests were often given handsome robes or gold rings as farewell presents. Gold and silver were used extensively for jewelry, and were also shaped into military helmets, and decorative animals—usually bulls and rams—for the temple. Jewels were sometimes buried with their dead owners. In the Royal Cemetery at Ur, gold and silver ornaments and other jewelry were found in large quantities. In one of their myths, the Sumerians tell of a god-king of Uruk who called upon the city of Aratta to show its surrender by sending him gold, silver, and precious stones.

As they developed their civilization, the wealth of the Sumerians also led to forms of greed which proved their undoing. By 2400 B.C. they had had many tyrants, corrupt officials, and selfish individuals. These bad times were relieved for a while when a city-king named Urukagina helped the poor and ended evil taxes. But the reign of Urukagina, who was king of the city of Lagash, lasted only ten years. In one of the many wars which the cities of Sumer waged against each other he was defeated by the king of Umma.

As a result of these petty wars, Sumerian cities rose and faded. Over a period of about a thousand years, first one city, then another, would be victorious. During the twenty-fourth century B.C., Sargon of Akkad, king of an area north of Sumer, conquered all the Sumerian cities. Soon he was master of the whole stretch of plains between the

This detail from the so-called "Royal Standard" of Ur shows feast in progress in the top panel while captured bullocks and asses are led to the palace.

Golden helmet from a rich citizen's grave shows the knotted hairdo that Sumerians wore during a battle.

Tigris and Euphrates reaching to the Persian Gulf. It is believed that he may even have conquered as far as present-day Lebanon. His was the first empire in the history of the world. But his descendants could not hold on to it, and by 2200 B.C. the Sargonid empire collapsed.

The period which followed was confusing and turbulent. "Who was king and who was not king?" a later historian asked when he wrote of these times. Then, about 2100 B.C., Ur-Nammu of Ur, who called himself King of Sumer and Akkad, became ruler. He built great temples at several Sumerian cities. At Ur, his temple was eighty feet high, 200 feet long, and 140 feet wide.

The kings who followed him continued his good works for about a hundred years. This is the time, remembered in the Old Testament, when Abraham was born in Ur. But when the rulers who followed King Ur-Nammu died, Sumer began to die, too. A poet who lived at the time started a poem with the words, "O thou city of high walls, thy land has perished."

Ur and its kingdom fell around 2025 B.C. About two hundred years later, Sumer and Akkad were made part of the Old Babylonian Kingdom. Hammurabi, the first great king of Babylon, is known to history as the author of a great Code of Laws. Actually, they are variations of the laws and practices of the Sumerians, who hundreds of years earlier had formed a bridge between early man and modern man.

CHAPTER 5

THE INDUS
Man Builds Cities

At about the time the cities of Sumer were being built in the Fertile Crescent, village tribes from the hills of what is now Pakistan started to move south. Like their fellow men to the west, they stopped at the banks of a river. This one, called the Indus, flows into the Arabian Sea. In a short time these men learned how to build dikes and drain the fields. Soon other villagers migrated into the valley, bringing with them some of the skills they learned from Sumerian traders. Sometime before 2500 B.C., the Indus valley became the birthplace of another early civilization.

The cities along the Indus were fabulous by the standards of ancient history, and would be remarkable even today. The two we know most about, Mohenjo-daro on the lower Indus, and Harappa, four hundred miles to the northeast, were intelligently laid out cities. They had wide streets, rectangular blocks, and efficient drainage systems. Each city covered an area of six or seven miles and could house from 20,000 to 50,000 people.

The houses in these cities were built of baked brick made in two standard sizes. They were probably molded in large quantities and hardened in kilns. Mortar was used to hold the bricks together. The Indus masons worked so well that excavated parts of their cities still stand today.

Foundations for a four-room house are revealed after excavation. Remains of a long hall are seen at right. The rooms appear large here, but were actually small

The design of the cities has convinced scientists that they were built according to a central plan. This has led to two further conclusions: that the Indus society must have had a strong government, perhaps led by a priest-king, and that it must have been prosperous. In the center of each city stood a raised citadel. The one at Mohenjo-daro had a

Bronze tools and weapons of the Indus civilization

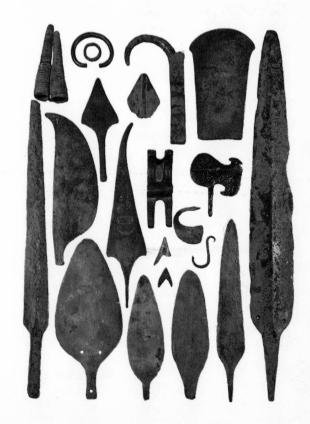

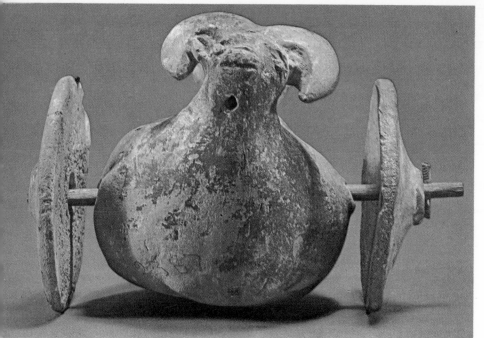

A ram on wheels (left) and the cart (below) are typical of the hundreds of children's toys found among ruins of Indus cities. Animals were very popular subjects with the artisans, and were fashioned with great care.

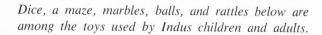

Dice, a maze, marbles, balls, and rattles below are among the toys used by Indus children and adults.

platform forty to fifty feet high and a base four hundred by two hundred feet. The citadel may have been used for protection during floods. It held a vast storehouse for grain, a brick-walled public bath, and what may have been an assembly hall. It probably held the offices of government officials as well.

The wealth of the Indus civilization is indicated by the kinds of toys and jewelry archaeologists have found. Indus craftsmen made costume jewelry in copper, bronze, semiprecious stones, gold, silver, and clay. The jewelry seems to have been worn by both men and women.

Toys were made for adults and children, and ranged from dice and marbles to maze games. Although many of these articles were probably used in trade, enough were found in the Indus valley to show that these luxuries were enjoyed at home as well.

Another form of luxury is found in the Indus sculpture. Most are figures of birds and animals—squirrels, rams, monkeys, doves—which were made with great skill. As with the art of earlier man, human figures are not nearly as well done as the animals. Some of the Indus animals may have

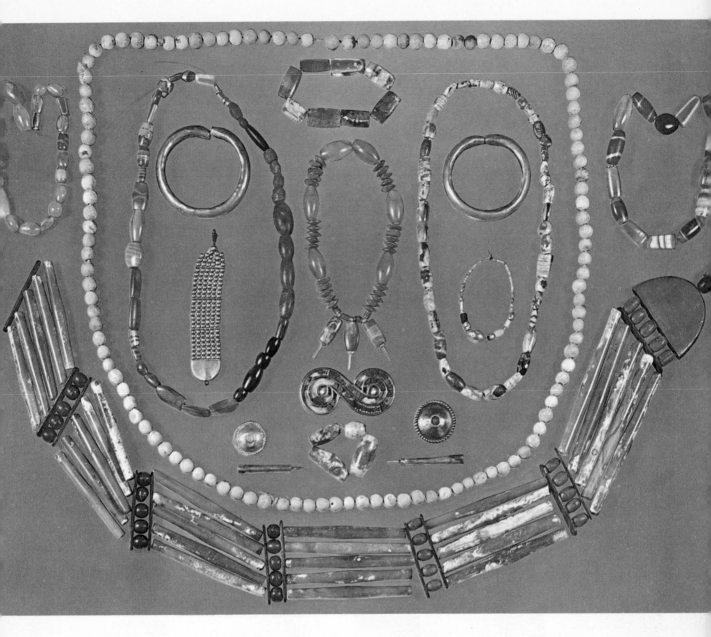

Indus jewelry was worn by both men and women. Beads, earrings, and head ornaments were made of many materials.

been used in forms of worship, and others for ornaments. But most seem to have been designed as toys. Some had mountings for wheels; others had holes for strings which could make animal heads waggle. In Chanhu-daro, a city eighty miles south of Mohenjo-daro, archaeologists have found large shops and clay kilns where these statues must have been turned out by the hundreds.

The people of the Indus valley were as advanced in some of their ways as the Sumerians. They had weights scaled in some kind of decimal system, and linear measures not very different from our own inches and feet. They also had a form of writing. But unfortunately scientists have not yet been able to decipher it. It was basically picture writing, and used about 250 symbols and about 400 characters. Some numbers may have been used as well, but we can not be sure.

Examples of the writing have been found on a number of small seals made of steatite, a soft soapstone. Some of them appear to have a religious meaning. Of the many animals carved on them, one resembling the unicorn appears most often. Actually, the beast was probably an ox, which was a familiar object of worship in the ancient world. When the animal is carved in profile his two long

51

The crude figurines above probably represent a worshiper (second from right) and mother goddesses of the Indus religion. Goddess at extreme left carries holders on her head, probably for incense. Figure at far right may be costumed as wealthy Indus woman.

The flying dove below may have been a toy or figure for worship. It is designed to fit on a wooden pin.

52

horns appear as one, which may explain the legend of the unicorn.

Other religious forms include the pipal, or fig tree, and a three-headed figure. The fig tree is still sacred today to Buddhists and Hindus. The three-headed figure may have been the forerunner of Siva, one of Hinduism's important gods. Statues representing a mother goddess have also been found in the Indus valley. These may have embodied Indus ideas of creation and man's place among forces which he did not understand. The people of the Indus, unlike the Sumerians, do not seem to have had temples. They probably worshiped at home.

The skills with which the people of the Indus built their cities, their statues, and their jewelry could not be kept to themselves. Trade grew, and the influence of one large city spread to another, and then another. One of them, Lothal, was a port on the Arabian Sea southeast of the Indus itself. It had a sheltered harbor, into which two rivers

A waggling toy cow or bullock moves his head when the string is pulled. Many like it have been found.

flowed. And beyond the city were rich cotton and wheat fields. Between 2500 and 1500 B.C. Lothal was an important trading center. In addition to farm goods, it produced copper and beadwork and built and repaired ships.

At the height of its success the Indus civilization stretched along the coast of the Arabian Sea from modern Bombay to Karachi and beyond. Inland it reached some seven hundred miles to the northeast and three hundred miles to the west. It is not likely that this vast area was ruled as a single empire. It is more probable that each city was a separate unit, the way the Sumerian cities were. But although separate, they were held together by common customs.

Amazingly enough, considering the skills they developed early, the Indus cities did not improve much over the years. In ten centuries very little happened except that the cities grew larger. The art, the houses, and day-to-day life appear to have remained almost the same. No new ideas seem to have been introduced. In time, this lack of fresh activity brought an end to the Indus civilization.

A sacred bull, made of terra cotta, shows the care and precision with which Indus artisans made their animal figures. Human images were usually more crude.

*Indus seals (above) show pictographs and animals.
The carving (below) resembles a modern alley cat.*

Some scientists believe that when the forests were cut down to provide fuel to feed their brick ovens, the soil became eroded. Later, as the weather changed from wet to dry, the soil could not grow crops. Other scholars say the weather in this area has not changed much through the centuries. Whatever the reason, the Indus cities disappeared. The first to go were those in the north, the last those along the coast.

The final blow probably came by invasion. A wandering people, called Aryans, spread from the plateaus of Iran and from parts of what is now southeastern Europe. They came in waves at different times and covered an area from India to the eastern Mediterranean. They first appeared in the northern Indus area which is now called the Punjab.

We are not sure whether they conquered the Indus cities by sudden warfare or by slow infiltration. At Mohenjo-daro, skeletons have been found which show signs of people who were attacked and killed without warning. But this evidence is not present in other cities.

The conquerors did not have a taste for city life. Soon the major cities of the Indus were empty ruins. Later, other people moved into the ruins and lived among them. Some built houses of their own, but they were shoddy compared to the original Indus dwellings. The cities of the Indus dwindled out of history, victims of their own inability to change, of invasions and perhaps, in some cases, of floods.

A thousand years after the Indus civilization had died out, the conqueror Cyrus and his successor, Darius, built the great Persian empire. The Indus area was part of it when Alexander of Macedon conquered Persia in the fourth century B.C. The Greeks who marched with him marveled at the mighty rivers, at the sweet sugar cane, and at the cotton, which they thought was "wool" growing on trees. Except for influences felt by the later Hindu people of India, this seems to be the extent of the impression left on western civilization by the people of the Indus valley.

Magnificent stone figure (right) found at Mohenjo-daro may have been local Indus god or one of priest-kings who may have ruled the entire Indus region.

CHAPTER 6

EGYPT
Man Builds
a Nation

It is no accident that the first three great civilizations of the world rose on the banks of three mighty rivers. Of the three rivers, none was as bountiful as the Nile, which flowed west of the Red Sea toward the Mediterranean. Each summer the Nile overflowed its banks and left rich black earth behind. Here, the people who lived in the river valley could harvest two, and sometimes three, crops a year. Here, too, they were left alone in safety. Man had not yet ventured on the Mediterranean Sea to the north, or crossed the deserts to the east and west. And here, about 2700 B.C., the Old Kingdom of Egypt emerged out of a group of feuding tribes and villages which had existed for some four hundred years.

Although ancient Egypt lasted for nearly 3,000 years, and contributed many important ideas to the world, its two major achievements came early. The first was the idea of union. According to tradition, a southern king named Menes brought the divided tribes together into one nation. The second was the related idea of a divine king. Men had believed in gods before, but in Egypt the god was a visible ruler—a god-king who guided and unified. Together, these ideas produced a country

The temple of Queen Hat-shepsut nestles below the cliffs near Thebes. Built for the first woman ruler of Egypt, its beauty stands out against solid rock.

57

with a central government, technical skills, a useful written language, and a new style in art.

The Nile River made the idea of a united nation under a god-king possible. Herodotus, the famous Greek historian, once said that "anyone who sees Egypt...must perceive that it is an acquired country, the gift of the river." In many ways this is true. Along the Nile's fertile banks the ancient Egyptians clustered just as they do today. By use of irrigation ditches, its crop-producing area was extended from two to twenty miles in Upper Egypt and to one hundred and twenty miles near the Mediterranean. The ancient Egyptians not only had food enough for all, but a good deal more to trade for the things they lacked.

In addition to the Nile's bountiful gift of the soil, it unified the people because it was such an excellent highway for trade and communication. With sailboats and skiffs, Egyptian traders and government officials traveled from one city to another. The sense of union was thus continually strengthened.

Although it is not connected with the Egyptian union, another thing comes to us from the Nile—the division of our year into 365 days. This came about because the Egyptians noticed over a period of fifty years that the river rose fairly regularly. The time between these rises was recorded and found to average 365 days. From this the Egyptians developed the first sun calendar, which they divided into four seasons of 120 days each, plus five days.

The capital of the Old Kingdom of Egypt was Memphis, not far from today's city of Cairo. Here, tradition says, King Menes set up his government behind whitewashed ramparts. Under the first god-kings of Egypt there was no written code of law. The law was the king's will. In practice, this was not abused in Egypt's early days. The Egyptians believed in *ma'at,* a concept which held the seeds of the later idea of a "higher law." *Ma'at* combined the principles of order, justice, harmony, goodness, and truth. The king and all his officials were supposed to govern in accordance with it. When they

Prince Ra-hotep and his wife Nefret, a noble couple of the Old Kingdom, were portrayed for their tomb in lifelike statues pictured above. Rock crystal was used for the eyes of these painted limestone images that were uncovered by excavators in the year 1871.

Egyptian artists (left) adorn walls of a temple for the glory of their king. In foreground, the architect directs the work of draftsmen, sculptors, painters.

Osiris, eventually worshiped as god of the after-life

did, the danger of tyranny or dictatorship was less real than the one-man rule might indicate.

In a country as large as ancient Egypt, no king could rule without a large number of officials. Thus, though he was a god, many mortals had to carry out the duties of government. Soon there came into being ministers, governors, mayors, and a vast number of clerks, or scribes. But this did not bring with it a rigid caste system. The growing need for officials meant that young people of talent could rise even from the peasant classes.

The prosperity which came to the Egyptians showed itself in the way they lived. The rich usually built homes in the country beyond the big cities. They planted gardens, vineyards, and fruit orchards, and relaxed in the sun. The houses, made of brick and wood, faced north so they would get cool winds from the Mediterranean and avoid the hot winds from the desert. The windows were high, the rooms airy. In these homes, women enjoyed a special place of honor. The Egyptian queen herself was considered the wife, mother, and often the daughter of gods. On their tombs Egyptian men often included the portraits of their wives.

Although their homes were impressive when compared to those of earlier peoples, the Egyptians put their best artistic and technical skills into their tombs. This was a result of their belief in the immortality of their rulers. Their tombs were therefore to be their homes through all eternity, and had to be built of material that would last. The Egyptians used stone, of which they had a great abundance. White limestone, red and gray granite, black and green diorite, and white, peach, and rose alabaster were cut into huge blocks. From these the great pyramids were formed, many of which still stand securely on the desert sands.

Building these huge tombs took feats of engineering which are marvels even today. The pyramid builders had no iron tools to cut the stone out of quarries. They had no wheels, pulleys, or work animals to carry, hoist, or drag the blocks, some of which weighed as much as forty-five tons. Their mathematics was crude by our standards. Yet each problem was solved. Soft rock, such as limestone, was cut with copper chisels and saws. Hard rock, like granite, was pounded into shape by even harder stone balls made of diorite. The blocks and columns were moved by men using sledges, ramps, rollers, and ropes. And the stones were fitted together in accordance with the engineers' mathematical formulas. In the Great Pyramid of Khufu, at Giza, the blocks of stone averaged two and a half tons each, and were laid with joints no larger than one fiftieth of an inch.

But with all their skills, the Egyptian engineers could not build without a large supply of manpower. For the royal monuments, all able-bodied men were expected to donate a few months of work each year. Later, foreign labor, including Hebrews, also worked on the pyramids. The workers were treated well, and received food, clothes, and housing while they were thus employed.

So much emphasis was put into life after death that the tombs became treasure houses. Into them were placed the things which had given the dead man pleasure on earth. Food, clothing, furniture, jewelry, and works of art were placed alongside written records of the man's life. Paintings showing him at work and play, with his companions, courtiers, and servants, were often used to decorate the tomb. For the very first kings, servants were put to death so they could serve their masters in the new life. The practice was later discontinued.

The belief in an after-life was probably due to the pleasures the Egyptians knew in real life. They simply felt that life in the next world would be more of the same. The scenes they had painted in their tombs show something of these feelings. Often there were scenes of abundant harvests, of the hunt, of feasts and games. And the Egyptians sometimes included touches of humor, too, such as an ape tripping up a servant.

After about five hundred years of prosperity and growth, the Old Kingdom of Egypt collapsed. There were many reasons for this. One scholar says that there was so much wealth, and so much effort spent in seeking it, that very few people worked for the common good. Also, the nobles in the cities far from the capital became stronger and more independent over the years. As this happened, succeeding kings became weaker and did not fulfill their duty to the nation as a whole. Also, so much labor and wealth went into building and furnishing the pyramids that trade declined.

For more than a hundred years, anarchy and civil war raged in Egypt. Then a time came when

mk	*wi*	*m*	*nfw*	*n·f-imy*
Behold,	I	(am as)	a skipper	belonging to him.

ḥm·n·(i)	*ꜥwy*	*grḥ*	*mi*	*hrw*
I am ignorant of	sleep	night	as well as	day.

Hieroglyphic sentences, spaced for clarity, are from tomb of a man who claimed to work hard for his king.

some of the rich who had begun to treat the peasants as slaves were scorned. A thousand years before the Hebrews and Greeks talked about human rights, Egyptians began to talk about the responsibility of rulers and the rights of the ruled. Some kind of free speech was even encouraged. Many who spoke out, including peasants, reminded the rulers that they had forgotten *ma'at*. That alone, one said, "lasts unto eternity." Only those who practice it, he added, are "remembered for goodness. That is the principle of the word of god."

Out of the turmoil came a feeling that all people who lived righteously—not just kings—would enjoy life after death. Middle-class families now

Painting of the 18th Dynasty depicts musicians and dancing girls. Perfume drips from musicians' heads as they play.

Painted relief of Tut-ankh-Amon and his queen shows how cluttered later empire art and dress had become.

started to imitate on a smaller scale the royal burials of the past. But since wealth, prestige, and rich offerings were no longer thought to be enough to guarantee the after-life, reforms of some of the worst abuses were eventually made.

As the reform movement started to make headway, Egypt was taken over by the rulers of the city of Thebes. This period lasted about three hundred years and is known as the Middle Kingdom. The Theban kings were strong, promoted public works, and brought a new prosperity. But the kings could never control all the provinces or the nobles who ruled them. This led to internal weaknesses, and exposed Egypt to its first conquest by foreigners.

The invaders were Asiatic tribesmen called Hyksos, or shepherd kings, who used horses and chariots, which the Egyptians had never seen. But the Hyksos had no talent as rulers, and after about a hundred years the Egyptians adopted their weapons and drove them out.

About 1600 B.C., the Egyptians embarked on a period which we call the New Kingdom. It is from this time that the title of "pharaoh" began to apply to the Egyptian kings. It had been used before to mean the king's palace. One of the greatest of the pharaohs in the New Kingdom was a woman, Queen Hat-shepsut. She took the throne at the death of her husband Thut-mose II, and set about helping Egypt recover from the results of the Hyksos occupation. She encouraged traders to travel to distant lands and sponsored great buildings at home. One of the most beautiful temples ever built was erected in her honor near Thebes.

Despite the efforts of Queen Hat-shepsut, the years of conquest had brought deep changes to Egyptian life. Instead of the joyous spirit that had once existed, the people lived in fear of another invasion. The pharaohs became stricter in their rule, and helped by their priests, imposed strong discipline. The rights of individual human beings became lost in a silent obedience to the needs of national security.

At the same time, the Egyptians also set about conquering the lands near them. After Queen Hat-shepsut's death, Pharaoh Thut-mose III led armies against the city-kings of Palestine, Syria, and Lebanon. Nearly every spring for twenty years he marched off to fight in Asia. He had great military talent and won many victories. Under him Egypt's empire reached its highest peak.

During the centuries of rise and fall, the Egyptians worshiped many gods. Sometimes the emphasis on different gods changed suddenly as the

Gold statuette, eight inches tall, of the god Amon dates from the 22nd Dynasty. He was considered the most powerful god. The scimitar stands for "life."

Colossi of Amen-hotep III, six stories high, tower above flooding Nile River.

rulers changed. Sometimes it changed gradually as villages joined to become cities, and the people brought their local gods into a kind of unity. In a town named Behdet, for example, people worshiped a god in the form of a falcon they called Horus. In another town, Osiris was first worshiped as the god of vegetation. Eventually, they were brought together with others to form a family of gods. This in turn led to a host of legends which accounted for the birth and lives of the gods.

Under the Theban kings, Thebes became capital of the Egyptian empire, and Amon-Re became the most powerful god of all. The people of Thebes had worshiped as a local god, Amon, god of the invisible wind. All Egyptians respected Re, the sun god. The Theban kings combined Amon and Re into one god with power over sun and air. He was so important the priests of Amon-Re became nearly as powerful as the pharaohs themselves.

Yet it was not until a pharaoh named Amen-hotep IV took power in the fourteenth century B.C. that an effort was made to honor one god alone. He chose Aton, which had been considered

The head of Ramses II lies on the ground amid the ruins of a temple he built around 1280 B.C. for the glory of Amon and himself. The head is 12 feet tall.

the resting place of Re, as the single god. Aton, he said, was the source of life, love, and joy in the universe. Amen-hotep changed his name to Akh-en-Aton, which means "He Who is Serviceable to Aton." He moved the capital from Thebes to a new city which he called Akhet-Aton, which means "The Place of the Effective Glory of Aton." Here he built a great temple and many smaller chapels.

Akh-en-Aton's efforts to change the religion of Egypt were in vain. The priests rebelled at his idea of one god, and this conflict weakened the empire. Although Akh-en-Aton's idea failed, it may have influenced Moses, who grew up in Egypt. After Akh-en-Aton's death, the empire was rebuilt once more, but it was never again to have the glory and power of its early days. Ramses II built many obelisks, giant statues, and, at Thebes, a colossal hall of columns. But it was a hollow glory. Enemies of Egypt stood ready to conquer the land.

There were many invasions—by the Ethiopians, Babylonians, Assyrians, and Persians. Finally, in 322 B.C., Alexander the Great conquered Egypt and established Ptolemy as his own pharaoh. Under Ptolemy there was a brief period of greatness. The library at Alexandria became the center of world learning. Then, with the death of Cleopatra in 30 B.C., the Egyptian empire faded at last.

CHAPTER 7

THE MEDITERRANEAN
Mingling of Nations

Until about the year 2000 B.C., the two major civilized groups of men in the world knew very little about each other. The early Sumerians and the early Egyptians built their own cities and cultivated the land nearest them. They traded among themselves and rarely ventured beyond familiar territory. Then, when Babylonia succeeded Sumer, and Egypt had been reunited by the Theban kings, a new movement started. People from one nation met those from another. They swapped ideas as well as products, and each benefited. The area where they met became the springboard for civilization's leap to Europe. It was a narrow strip of land along the eastern end of the Mediterranean Sea. From it came some of the most important ideas in the history of mankind.

This piece of coastline, which today includes parts of Syria, Lebanon, Israel, and western Jordan, was on the land route between Asia and Africa. More important, its ports connected those two continents with Europe. In time, nearly every important group of people in the ancient world stopped there, and for 1,500 years there was a lively mingling of people with different backgrounds and experiences.

The descendants of the early settlers along this strip were called Canaanites, and later, Phoenicians. Both names come from the color purple because these people were famous for a royal purple dye which they obtained from shellfish. Canaan was probably a neighboring tribe's word for "purple dye"; Phoenician comes from the Greek word *phoinix* which means "purple red." Under neither name did they ever achieve great political or military power. But they were great craftsmen, traders, and colonizers. Because of these skills they may have had a greater influence on Europe than any other people who came to the eastern shores of the Mediterranean.

The Phoenician ships seemed to be everywhere. In *The Odyssey,* Homer mentioned the arrival of one fleet in these words, "Thither come Phoenicians, men famed for their ships, greedy knaves, bringing countless trinkets in their black ship." The poet's use of "greedy knaves" may simply be envy of the Phoenicians' success in trading. There was no question that they were the leading merchants of their time.

The main home ports of the Phoenician ships were the cities of Tyre, Sidon, and Byblos. Near these cities stood forests thick with tall cedar trees. The Phoenicians fashioned the lumber from the forests into the finest, strongest, and sturdiest ships men had ever seen.

A Phoenician warehouse on the waterfront at Tyre is packed with export goods. Phoenician traders carried ideas as well as goods to the Mediterranean lands.

At the harbor of Tyre, shipwrights (left) work with slaves to shape the ribs of a merchant ship. On the right,

timber-bearing slaves are directed by a soldier. Behind, at dockside, longshoremen load goods onto ships.

69

The Phoenicians commanded crews of slave oarsmen who carried them through unexplored waters to new and strange lands. They voyaged to Malta, Sicily, Sardinia, and through the Straits of Gibraltar to the Atlantic coast of Spain. Some scholars believe they may have traveled as far as Britain looking for raw materials. The Greek historian Herodotus credits them with a voyage around the continent of Africa.

The Phoenician cities became the busiest in the world. The shipyards were constantly turning out new vessels, the warehouses held vast stores of goods, and in the workshops men changed raw material into finished goods. When the ships left port they carried finely decorated plates and bowls of gold, silver, and bronze, copper ingots, bronze shields, iron daggers and spear points. Their wares included bottles made of ivory or pottery, filled with perfumes, and fine woolens and linens dyed red or purple. It is likely that purple became the color of royalty because the dye was so expensive that only kings could afford it.

In some of the lands in which the Phoenicians traded they merely set up a tent, sold their goods, and went on their way. Eventually, as they sailed greater distances, they established permanent colonies. These were started as small, fortified villages, many of which became major trading centers in their own right. One, founded on the Atlantic coast of Spain about 1100 B.C., became the modern city of Cadiz. Another, established about 950 B.C. on the North African coast near present-day Tunis, was called Carthage. In time, Carthage became a sea power itself and challenged the Etruscans, the Greeks, and finally the Romans, who destroyed the city.

The colonies the Phoenicians established were not to be the greatest gift they left behind. Above all, they are remembered as the inventors of the first true alphabet. The Phoenician businessmen needed a way to keep detailed, accurate records. Egyptian hieroglyphics were too clumsy. The Phoenicians changed the pictographs to symbols or letters which had a fixed sound value. Along with the goods they brought to other lands, the Phoenicians brought their new way of writing. Among the most receptive of the people they visited were the Greeks. The Roman alphabet we use today comes from the Greeks' adaptation of the Phoenician alphabet. The word "Bible" comes from the Phoenician port of Byblos, famous as an exporter of papyrus which was used for writing paper.

Although they were successful overseas, the Phoenicians could not hold on to large areas at home. In a way, they were forced to look to the sea because they were reduced to living in their port cities by a succession of inland invaders. At different times, the Hittites, the Assyrians, the Egyptians, and the Hebrews ruled the territory around them.

This detail of a Canaanite carving on an ivory panel shows the queen of Megiddo and a musician with lyre.

Phoenician alphabetic inscription surrounds name of Egyptian Pharaoh Osorkon I on this bust of 900 B.C.

The most important of the conquerors were the Hebrew tribes who, some time after 1400 B.C., overran part of the land of Canaan. They made their capital Shiloh, in the southern hills of Palestine, where they kept the Ark of the Covenant. Bound by a common faith in one God, the twelve tribes of Israel lived under a loose arrangement without a strong central government. They did not join to form the Kingdom of Israel until they were threatened by the Philistines. A local chieftain named Saul united the tribes, defeated the enemy, and was made the first king.

When Saul died in battle his son-in-law, David, became king. David completed the wars against the Philistines and started new conquests against Canaan. When he captured the city of Jerusalem he made it the capital of the kingdom. Under David, Israel became truly united, but it never attained the wealth of the Phoenician cities on the coast.

David's son and successor, Solomon, imitated the ways of the Phoenicians. He brought in Phoenician architects and craftsmen to build his palace and temple, Phoenician metalworkers to operate his copper mines, and Phoenician sailors to carry his goods. On Solomon's death, the Kingdom of Israel split into two nations—Israel and Judah. With this division the political power of the Hebrews declined.

Long before 600 B.C., the Hebrews, the Phoenicians, and the Egyptians were overrun by the conquering Assyrians, who ruled the entire region from the Persian Gulf to the Nile. The Assyrians were probably the greatest military power before the Roman Empire. They beat cities into submission, and usually pillaged and destroyed them before moving on. Occasionally, they would spare a city if the proper tribute were paid. Most of the Phoenician cities survived by paying the Assyrians heavily. The Assyrian domination lasted until 612 B.C. when the Chaldeans, Medes, and Persians conquered Nineveh, the Assyrian capital.

Except for the Hittites and Egyptians, most of the famous people of this time and place were Semites. The name comes from the Biblical account of the Flood and the supposed descent of the Hebrews from Noah's son Shem, or Sem. Scholars believe that the people in this part of the world, having come from the same general area, were racially related. Although this relationship was never allowed to interfere with the bloody battles they had, the Semites, separately or together, left an incredible heritage.

The author of a scholarly study of their civilization includes among their accomplishments: ". . . the very means whereby we express our thoughts in writing, the alphabet." And he follows with the Semites' great contribution to human thought, "The conception . . . of the oneness of God, of a single moral power." This "essential kernel of Hebrew religion" was carried to Europe by Christianity, and to Asia and Africa by Islam, the religion of Mohammed. Few people in ancient or modern times have donated as much to the world.

A copper refinery near the Red Sea is operated for King Solomon of Israel by Phoenicians. Ore is placed in clay pots which are set in red-hot charcoal pits.

CHAPTER 8

THE AEGEAN
Art and War

Until less than a hundred years ago, few people believed that the stories told by the Greek poet Homer had any basis in truth. The tales of gods, heroes, and events in *The Iliad* and *The Odyssey* were dismissed as legends made up to entertain the people of Greece. But in 1871 an amateur German archaeologist named Heinrich Schliemann found the site of the city that was Homer's Troy. And in 1899, Sir Arthur Evans, an English archaeologist, found the ruins of the fabulous palace of Minos on the island of Crete. Now scholars are convinced that two civilizations—the Minoan and the Mycenaean—were the forerunners by a thousand years of the great period of Greece. Furthermore, the history of these two peoples bears a striking resemblance to the stories that were told by Homer.

The Minoans lived on Crete, which is at the mouth of the Aegean Sea. Crete is about 160 miles long, and its northern coast has large bays which make excellent harbors. Its south coast, as Homer described it, "is a smooth cliff, sheer towards the sea." The people who lived on this island are called

The palace at Knossos, seat of power during Crete's golden age, is reached by a massive stone viaduct.

75

Minoans after a legendary king named Minos. Until about 2500 B.C. they lived in caves and huts without any of the skills which other men had acquired in Asia and Africa. At that time, the island was discovered by wandering sailors who proceeded to change the island's way of life.

Since it was an ideal central spot for trading, ships were built and goods carried to other Mediterranean ports. By 2000 B.C. potters were turning out gaily colored vases, and wheeled vehicles had been introduced. More people came to settle, some of whom brought the idea of writing, which was widely used by Minoan businessmen. In the course of this growth three great palaces were built. One rose in the south of the island, and another on the northern coast. The third and greatest palace crowned Knossos in north-central Crete. The ruins of the palace at Knossos still stand today as a monument to this period, known as the Age of the Old Palaces. Then, in 1700 B.C., the palaces and most of the island's towns were destroyed, probably by an earthquake.

The Minoan vase (at left), carved from steatite, shows harvesters following leader wearing fringed mantle.

Bull leaping, seen in fresco below, was a favorite sport on the island of Crete from 2000 to 1400 B.C.

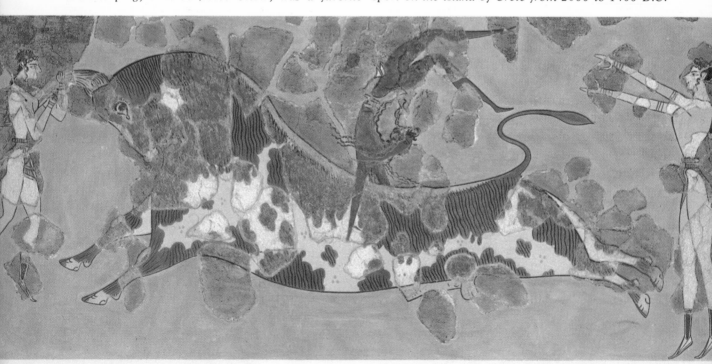

The Minoans were not defeated. They rebuilt better than before, and started what has been called the Age of the New Palaces. The most important of the new ones was that of Minos at Knossos. It was a tremendous and elaborate building with great mazes of apartments, corridors, colonnades, light wells, and staircases. It rambled over more than six acres, and was built of masonry, rubble, and wood to a height of three stories. Throughout the palace were brightly painted pillars and walls.

Around the palace grew an important city. Or, as Homer put it: "One of the ninety towns of Crete is a great city called Knossos, and there, for nine years, King Minos ruled and enjoyed the friendship of almighty Zeus." We do not know for sure, but it is thought that one or more Cretan kings used the name of Minos, or that it may have been a royal title, like pharaoh or Caesar.

On an island with a natural wealth of agricultural products and natural harbors for shipping, prosperity was inevitable. One ancient writer called Crete "great, fat and well-fed," the Isle of the Blessed. The prosperity permitted time for the pleasures of life, and the Minoans developed a zest

Throne room in Palace of Minos (above) still has its alabaster throne. The frescoes depict mythical griffins. Broken religious objects found on floor suggest prayer offerings during 1500 B.C. disaster.

A drinking cup in the shape of a bull (right) found at Knossos reflects the chief Minoan symbol. Zeus, legendary father of Minos, was said to have taken the form of a white bull in order to kidnap Europa.

77

A harvesters' procession, patterned after the vase on page 76, makes its way through great central courtyard

of the Palace of Minos. The ceremony was a form of thanksgiving to the gods of nature for a bountiful season.

Mycenaean warriors battle outside a walled city. Soldiers in foreground fight over the body of a fallen attacker.

for sport and art. The most popular sport was bull-leaping, in which, without any weapons, young boys and girls defied a charging bull. A youngster would pull himself over the bull's body by grasping its horns, and then perform a somersault as the animal passed below.

Unlike most people of the ancient world, the Minoans did not build temples or monuments to their gods. Many of their homes had tiny spaces for prayers, but the main places of worship were natural. A mountain peak, a forest grove or, most popular of all, a cave were the usual choices of the Minoans. To these places the Minoans brought their offerings.

One of these caves, with its intricate passageways, may have given rise to the myth of Theseus. In this story, the city of Athens was required to send at regular intervals seven young men and seven young women to be fed to the Minotaur, a beast with a bull's head on a man's body. The Minotaur was kept in a labyrinth from which it was impossible to find one's way back. Theseus volunteered to be a human sacrifice. He killed the Minotaur and, with the help of a long string which he had unwound as he entered the labyrinth, was able to find his way back.

The story of Theseus may have been made up to explain the end of the Minoan period. After

His foes try to take his weapons and armor, while his friends try to drag him away for honorable burial.

1600 B.C., the Mycenaeans on the mainland of Greece began to dominate the Aegean area. They may have ruled Crete as well. For it is the blending of these two people which seems to have produced the great Greek period which was to come later. By the time the Minoan cities and palaces were destroyed by another earthquake, in 1500 B.C., Mycenae was the most important city in Greece; it remained so for three hundred years.

Those were the years of which Homer wrote. The real-life counterparts of Odysseus, Menelaus, and King Agamemnon were a brave and intelligent people. Their fighting skills have been verified by the recent deciphering of their writing. Their artistry and craftsmanship have been shown by the beautiful objects found in the ruins of their buildings. Archaeological findings—which are still being made—indicate that the life described by Homer was a reasonably accurate description of Mycenae, its people, and its events. The Trojan War may not have been fought to free Helen who was held captive in Troy, as Homer told it. It is more likely that the Greeks sailed across the Aegean and besieged Troy in order to free their trade routes to the Black Sea. Whatever the reason, a lengthy war did take place and a city on the site of Homer's Troy was destroyed about the time that he says it was.

81

According to Greek legend, Mycenae was built by Perseus, who had slain the Gorgon Medusa. Modern archaeologists believe it was founded by some tribes about 3000 B.C. It was strategically located at the mouth of several mountain passes which gave it great security. It was surrounded by fertile fields which bore figs, olives, grapes, barley, and other crops. Beyond the fields were copper mines. By the end of the thirteenth century B.C., Mycenae was dominated by a gigantic palace, surrounded by walls sixty feet high and twenty feet thick. It was reached by a long road ascending from the rich Argive plain. Inside were fine apartments, a beautiful throne room, and a great hall decorated with military scenes.

The protection provided by the palace's giant walls was necessary in Mycenae. Warfare was almost a constant part of the lives of the Mycenaeans. Because the mountains and the sea broke Greece up into so many small areas, the cities were separate units. They were, in fact, city-states, long before later Greece was divided that way. The men of one city fought those of another in defense of their small plots of land. They also fought for honor and glory. "In ancient times," wrote the Greek historian Thucydides, "all Hellenes carried weapons."

There were no fixed battlefields for group warfare or arenas for individual combat, as there were to be later. Instead, fighting was done wherever the enemy was found. Occasionally, duels were arranged between heroes from each side. Weapons and equipment were made by individual soldiers for their own use. Some favored leather, others bronze. Helmets came from a wide variety of materials, including boars' teeth. A soldier was also protected by his great shield, often shaped like a figure eight, which covered him from the neck to below the knees. But it was so heavy that a fallen fighter was often pinned beneath it.

Besides fighting, the Mycenaeans displayed their courage and prowess in hunting. Often this was done for the sport itself, but sometimes it arose from necessity. Bears, wolves, and lions lived in the mountains and often attacked flocks and human beings in the fields and villages below.

Whether in battle or in hunting, death was a commonplace event in Mycenae. It did not warrant mourning, especially if a man died bravely. This was considered the proper fulfillment of a hero's life. Later, as the influence of the Egyptians reached them, the Mycenaeans started to think about an after-life. When this happened they began to build elaborate tombs for their heroes and kings. Although the Mycenaeans decorated them with fine art and furnished them well, their tombs did not achieve the grandeur of the Egyptian tombs.

By the late thirteenth century B.C. the Mycenaeans went into a decline. The reasons for this are

obscure. A number of invasions on the Greek mainland had taken place, and new people were pushing in. A group of tribes known as the Sea People brought great upheavals throughout the Mediterranean area. They raided merchant ships, among them those of the Mycenaeans. With their trade routes cut, the Mycenaean cities turned on each other.

This is probably the time that Mycenae sailed across the Aegean to attack Troy. But even that victory was not enough. From central Greece and the northwest mountains came the Dorians, bringing new chaos to a sick land. Mycenae crumbled and died physically, but was reborn to live forever in the great tales of Homer.

Three lions are shown in a hunt scene on a bronze dagger blade with an inlay of gold and silver. As two lions flee, a third strikes down a huntsman.

Bodies of a king and queen lie on floor of tomb as mourners watch. Behind, fire consumes perishable offerings.

CHAPTER 9

THE ETRUSCANS
Gay, Gifted People

By 1000 B.C. the most vigorous of the peoples in the eastern Mediterranean started to move west. The Greeks and the Phoenicians, looking for raw materials for their craftsmen and buyers for their goods, roved the length of the Mediterranean. They established colonies on the shores of northern Africa and southern Europe. In this way the knowledge of the east was spread to new lands and influenced the people who lived there. But none of these colonies developed a civilization of its own. The only truly new civilization to come out of the westward movement was that of the Etruscans, a highly talented people who founded their society around 800 B.C. on the western coast of Italy.

No one knows for sure where the Etruscans came from. They may have arrived in a body from one of the coastal areas of Asia Minor, or they may have developed from tribes in Italy's interior who moved to the coast and mixed with immigrants from the east. The Greek historian Herodotus, who wrote of the Etruscans in the fifth century B.C., said they came from Lydia in Asia Minor, which they left because of a famine. They

Etruscan fresco found in the Tomb of the Leopards depicts the dead enjoying food and drink with friends in the life they expected in the afterworld.

85

A burial urn (above) of the seventh century B.C. is the container for man's weapons, woman's jewels, or whatever else survivors thought the dead might need.

This fond couple (right) is carved on the lid of a funeral urn. Upper-class Etruscan women enjoyed an equality with men that was rare in ancient times.

A stone chair (below) stands in the vestibule of a huge tomb at Cerveteri. The shield above the chair, like the rooms of the tomb, was carved from rock.

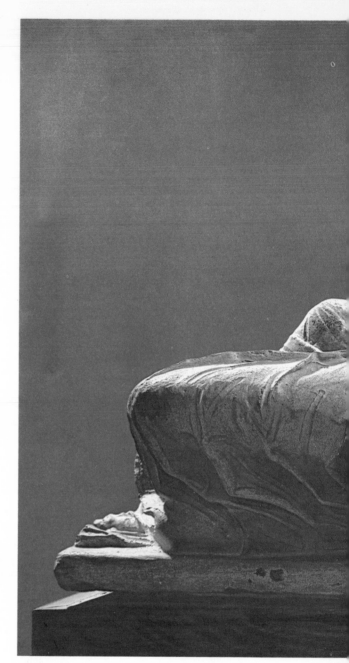

were led, he wrote, by a prince named Tyrrhenos. From this, Herodotus called these people Tyrrhenoi, or Tyrrhenians. The Romans later referred to them as Tusci or Etrusci, which is the basis of the name we use today. The Greek term lives on in the waters off the coast of Etruria, which are still called the Tyrrhenian Sea.

Wherever they came from, the Etruscans were affected by the warm climate and the rugged terrain of Italy. These natural elements, plus the vigor and genius of the people who came together in Etruria, produced a civilization of great importance. It not only influenced Italy, but through

trade and travel across the Italian Alps helped speed the movement of people in Europe from barbarism to civilization. The Roman Empire which came later owed much to the early Etruscans.

Although it used the Greek alphabet, the Etruscan language was different from all known languages. As a result, the written records of the Etruscans are not much help to us in studying their history. Scholars have worked out many words on separate documents, but have learned nothing of real value. Most of the words have been found on tombs and do not tell us more than the dates and names of places and people.

Our basic knowledge of the Etruscans comes from Greek and Roman historians. Unfortunately, they were not always objective in their accounts. The Greeks were jealous of the Etruscans, who kept them from expanding in the Mediterranean. In the Greek view, the Etruscans often appear to be thieves and pirates who spent their lives in riotous living. Until their own empire was established later, the Romans considered the Etruscans their rivals and enemies. The poem "Horatio at the Bridge" tells of a battle between the Romans and the Etruscans, who were led by Tarquin, their king.

Despite the Greek and Roman prejudices, their accounts do give us the formal history of the Etruscans. The first cities they built were probably Vetulonia and Populonia on the Italian coast opposite the island of Elba. From these, the Etruscans expanded along the coast and inland until there were twelve cities. The largest of them may not have held more than five or six thousand people, but that was sizable for the period.

The twelve cities were linked by mutual interests into a unit which modern scholars call "the Etruscan League." Between 700 and 500 B.C., the League expanded. Cities were founded as far north as the Po Valley, east to the Adriatic, south toward present-day Rome, and on the island of Corsica. At one time or another, there were forty-seven Etruscan cities.

As they expanded, the Etruscans made allies of Carthage, the African colony founded by the Phoenicians. They fought together to keep the Greeks from taking over the Mediterranean trade. In 540 B.C., a fierce naval battle took place between these rivals off Alalia, the Etruscan city on Corsica. The Greeks claimed a great victory, but theirs is the only account of the event and it may not be altogether accurate, since not long after the battle they abandoned Corsica. They probably would not have done so had they really won, because Corsica was rich in metals which were highly prized. The Etruscans established a new city on Corsica called Victory, and sought new conquests.

The Etruscans were great fighters. A good deal of their prowess was due to the arms and armor they fashioned of metal. The west coast of Italy and the off-shore islands supplied iron, copper, tin, and other metals in great quantities. The existence of these metals led to constant conflicts with the Greeks and other Mediterranean peoples.

Chariot racing, as shown in the frieze below, was a popular spectacle in the arenas of the Etruscan cities.

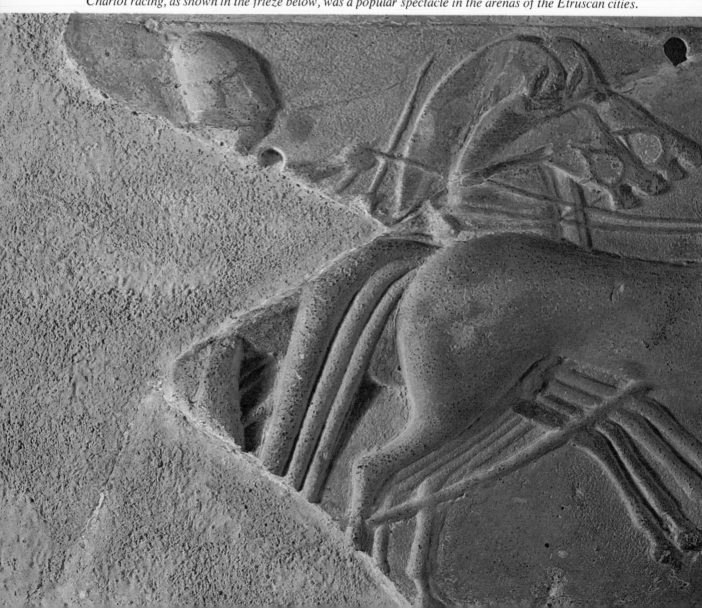

But none of them fashioned the metals into such superb weapons as did the Etruscans.

The Etruscans fought with battle axes, lances, and daggers, often from bronze, horse-drawn chariots. Their cavalry was finely armored and terrified the enemy. Perhaps the greatest contribution the Etruscans made to warfare was the formation of their infantrymen. Well armed for offense and protected by bronze helmets, shields, and shin guards, the men moved forward as a unit. Later, the Romans borrowed this formation as the basis for the legions with which they conquered their own enemies.

Metal was also the source of Etruscan wealth. Etruscan craftsmen were masters at working all the metals they discovered. They probably did more than any of the other early peoples to make iron popular. Whether of iron, copper, gold, or bronze, the beautiful and practical objects made

Statue of diver shows Etruscan mastery of anatomy.

by the Etruscans were in great demand. A substantial trade based on this metalwork led to Etruscan supremacy of the seas for a time. Etruscan merchant ships roved the Mediterranean, while a strong navy protected Etruscan routes and ports.

The wealth which poured into the Etruscan cities as a result of this extensive trade was spent mostly on pleasure. The Etruscans lived extremely well, which led to jealous comments by Greek and Roman historians. "Twice a day," said Diodorus Siculus, a Roman writer, "sumptuous tables are laid and everything brought that goes with exaggerated luxury—flowers, robes, and numerous silver goblets of various shapes; nor is the number of slaves who are in attendance small." It is likely that this kind of life was limited to the upper classes. The Etruscans maintained a rigid social system. Merchants, workers, and slaves could not rise above their position as they sometimes did in Greece and Rome.

Wealth was also reflected in the clothes the Etruscans wore, and the pride they took in them. Men usually wore short jackets or tunics. In cold

Etruscan farmer, yoked oxen are sculpted in bronze.

and died to music. Their favorite instruments were the stringed lyre, the curved trumpet and, most of all, the double flute. A Greek historian wrote that they used the flute while hunting, to lure animals into traps with "the purest and most harmonious melody." The Etruscan soldiers developed a war dance in which the rhythm was supplied by lances beaten in cadence against shields. Other dances were designed for pure pleasure. Single dancing girls or chorus groups of men and women were often hired as entertainers. The Greek philosopher Aristotle took a dim view of the Etruscan attitude toward music. They "fight, knead dough and beat their slaves to the sound of the flute," the philosopher wrote.

weather these were covered with a *tebennos,* a cloak which was very much like the later Roman toga. Women wore a light, pleated tunic and a thick outer cloak, often dyed in brilliant colors. Both men and women wore shoes made of leather or embroidered cloth which were long, pointed, and curled at the toes in the style worn in Asia Minor. Occasionally these would be replaced by ankle boots and sandals. The early Etruscans wore their hair long, and the men grew beards. But around 500 B.C. men began to shave and to cut their hair. Women shortened their hair as well and wore it in tight curls that framed the face, or tucked it behind their necks.

From what we know from written accounts and paintings, the Etruscans ate, danced, hunted, raced,

The Etruscans were also great sportsmen. On a single day at one of the popular Etruscan arenas, spectators could see chariot and horse races, foot races, pole vaulting, wrestling and boxing, acrobatics and trick riding. Sometimes there were even clowns to amuse the crowd. The horses which gave the Etruscans a strong cavalry were bred for racing as well. In addition to regular flat races, the Etruscans developed a game that is called *truia,* in which horses had to race over a course shaped like a maze.

The most elaborate games were staged at the funerals of the wealthy. In addition to a regular sports program, there were often duels to the death between two fighters, usually slaves. One variation of this was to have a man armed with a cudgel, but blinded by a sack over his head, fight a ferocious dog. These funeral rites were adopted by the Romans and eventually led to the mortal contests

Wrestlers lock hands over basins which go to winner.

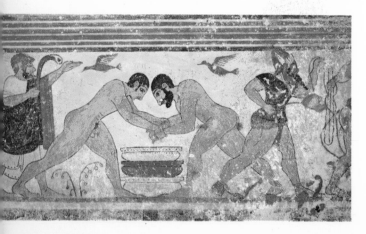

Etruscan foot race shows influence of Greek sports.

A golden brooch has interlaced palm leaves framing five lions on the top disk. It was found in a tomb.

what to expect of life. As a result, they were constantly trying to interpret the wills of the gods they worshiped. High priests made decisions based on lightning, thunder, and the entrails of sacrificed animals. The priests, called *haruspices,* were the forerunners of the Roman augurs, or readers of signs.

The Etruscans believed that every event on earth was of divine origin. Their religion, they felt, came to them from Tages, a spirit with the face of a child but the wisdom of an old man. Many of their other gods were closely related to those of the Greeks—Aplu to Apollo, Artums to Artemis, Hercle to Herakles. Their chief god, Tinia, resembled the Greek Zeus and the Roman Jupiter. His wife was like the Greek Hera and the Roman Juno.

In spite of their religion, their great wealth, and their military prowess, the Etruscans faded out of history. After they had kept Corsica from the Greeks they attempted to establish cities in southern Italy. The Greeks sought to prevent this, and in 524 B.C. at Cumae, not far from modern Naples, defeated the Etruscans. For the next century, the Etruscans were stopped in nearly every effort they made toward expansion. The emerging Romans,

Two-headed bird with four legs is mounted on wheels in imitation of a chariot. It is fashioned of bronze.

between professional gladiators which were popular in the Roman Empire.

The funeral games were in keeping with the Etruscan attitude toward death. The idea of death was a constant one among Etruscans, and they prepared for it as if it were to be a continuation of the life they knew. This led to the creation of "houses of the dead," which were replicas of those in which the Etruscans lived. Wealthy Etruscans had these rooms built on the outskirts of their cities. In them were placed the treasures the Etruscans had enjoyed in life—armor, pottery, ornaments. Sometimes frescoes depicting the dead man at war, sport, or the banquet table were painted on the walls.

While they seemed certain about what death would bring, the Etruscans were less sure about

Naked lancer in bronze at left is a fifth century depiction of Etruscan warrior. In offensive warfare the Etruscans used heavy lances with iron or bronze points, javelins, swords, sabers, daggers, and axes.

Samnites from the Italian hills, Celts from the north, and Greeks from Syracuse held them in check. A period of decline set in, and by 250 B.C. the Etruscans had submitted to the Romans.

But if the Etruscan culture ceased to exist as a separate entity, its influence lived on. It was not only that the golden crown, the golden ring and scepter which originated with them became the symbols of power for the Roman Empire. "These people," a French scholar has written, "were an active civilising agent in the heart of Italy....The true beginnings of Rome are to be found in their presence on the seven hills. Rome rid herself at an early date of the Etruscan tyrants, but she preserved a great part of their heritage. And the hatred Rome bore Etruria for centuries must not lead us to underestimate the importance of the debt owed to Etruria by Rome. The Etruscan influence was to live on in Rome in her Constitution ...in her religious thought and in the arts; it was to form part of the cultural heritage which Rome, in her turn, would leave to the West."

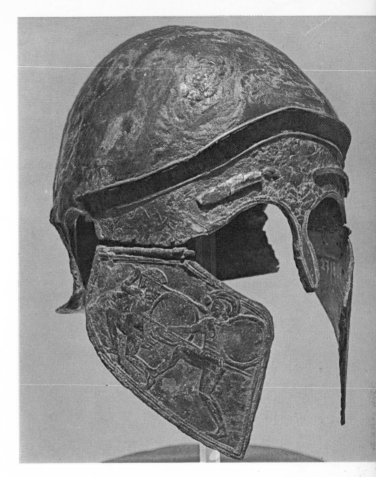

Ceremonial helmet is of the kind worn by Etruscan warriors for parades and other display occasions.

War chariot, reconstructed from bronze fragments, is fine example of the care with which Etruscans made their armor.

CHAPTER 10

CELTS AND SCYTHIANS
Wandering Tribes

Back of bronze mirror
discovered in England

While the people on the shores of the Mediterranean and in the Middle East settled in cities to develop new ways of living, those to the north remained wanderers. Traveling in tribes, these nomads ranged the forest lands and plains from western Europe to the borders of China. The Greeks and Romans called these people "barbarians," by which they meant people who lived beyond civilization.

Numerous so-called barbarian tribes appeared briefly and then vanished from history. Some settled peaceably on the lands to the south and became absorbed by the advanced civilizations they found. Others came as conquerors, overthrew existing cities and states, and wandered on. Still others, like the Hittites, came to conquer and remained to found states of their own.

Although civilization reached northern Europe later than it did the Mediterranean area, some barbarian tribes knew many civilized skills as early as 1000 B.C. They picked them up in the cities they raided or through trading, and passed them on

to others. In this way, the civilization of the south spread northward to the rest of Europe and eastward to Asia.

The two main groups of barbarians were the Celts and the Scythians. The Celts roamed through western Europe, into parts of what are now Spain and France and the British Isles. The Scythians wandered over a vast stretch of land across the southern part of what is now Russia. Although their areas did not cross, the Celts and Scythians had much in common. It is likely that there were chance meetings, perhaps at some central point like Hungary, where information and goods were traded.

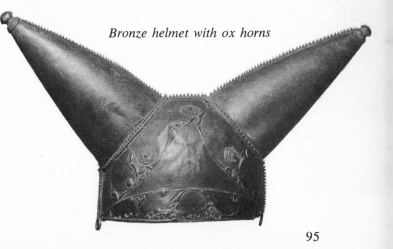

Bronze helmet with ox horns

A band of migrating Celts passes through rough land in search of a new home. Tribesmen carry belongings heaped in ox-drawn carts or strapped to their backs.

At a Celtic farmstead in southern Britain, a farmer raises his arm to greet a friend. According to Celtic custom, the friend is delivering his son to live here as a foster child, thus forming a bond between the families. The farmer's wattle-and-mud house stands at left. A woman, at right, ladles out grain

for bread from an underground storage pit. An abandoned pit, lower right, is filled with trash. In background, behind timber palisades, lie newly plowed fields. Around 850 B.C., many Celts gave up the wandering life to settle down, but farming never became as important as hunting and warfare for Celtic leaders.

In a sacred oak grove beside a pond, Celts gather to worship one of their deities. The chief Druid invokes the gods as offerings are cast on the water.

As they learned to make iron tools and weapons, many of the nomads gave up their roving life to settle down. The Celts started to do so about 850 B.C., which was several hundred years after the Hittites had learned to use iron. Oddly enough, northern Europe had greater sources of iron ore than the Middle East, but its people lagged in learning how to work it. When the Celts did learn, however, they used axes to cut down trees and build homes, and plows to farm the soil. This did not immediately change them into settlers, or cause them to build towns, however. For many years farming was only a temporary activity. Hunting and warfare—and the traveling which went with both—still came first.

Sometime during the second century B.C., the Celts began to form units which were almost towns or cities. In southern France and central Europe, a number of the tribes built houses near one another. The first hint that these settlements might be permanent, and perhaps even grow, was that the townspeople built forts to defend themselves. This was a major change in the Celtic way of life.

With settlement, the Celts improved their skills with iron. As the towns grew, the iron smith became one of the most important members of the community. He produced not only the iron swords and lances for battle, but also the plowshares and axes for farming. The smith was so highly regarded

A collar piece, worn by a Celt chieftain in Britain

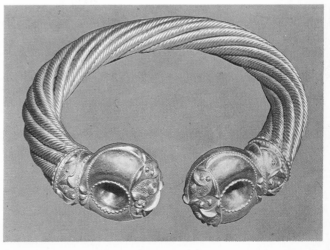

99

that the Celts considered him more a magician than a craftsman. For men, he made beautifully decorated shields and helmets, and for women, jewelry.

Living in towns did not cause the Celts to give up their warlike nature. Battles between tribes were constant. Yet with all their love of battle the Celts were not really good fighters. There was no doubt of their courage. They dashed into battle with wild shouts and the blowing of horns and trumpets. It was as if they counted on their daring, the noise, and the confusion to bring them to victory. But this did not always work.

Town defenders counted on stone or earthen forts, usually on hilltops, to keep enemies at bay. Some were built large enough to protect all the townspeople and their animals on the ground while the warriors fought from ramparts above. In intertribal battles, the forts usually held, but when the Celts were up against organized fighters they were easily defeated. The Romans, under Julius Caesar, had no trouble overcoming Celtic towns.

The Celts, ever since their nomadic days, were not tied together by any state or ruler. If anything gave them a sense of union it was a common religion based on belief in ancient tribal gods. These gods, the Celts felt, had magical powers over man, and their secrets were known only to a group of priests called Druids. Actually, the Druids, who had to study twenty years before they attained their positions, served as more than priests. They advised tribal chiefs, acted as judges in disputes, and were teachers of the young.

Under the direction of Druids, the Celts worshiped their gods in sacred groves and forest glades, usually near spring-fed pools of water. In Britain and Gaul, the oak tree, especially when decorated with mistletoe, was considered sacred. (The modern use of mistletoe at Christmas time goes back to this Celtic custom.) Quite often the Celtic religious rites involved human sacrifice. The Roman poet Lucan, writing in the first century A.D., told of trees "stained with human gore" on which no bird would perch.

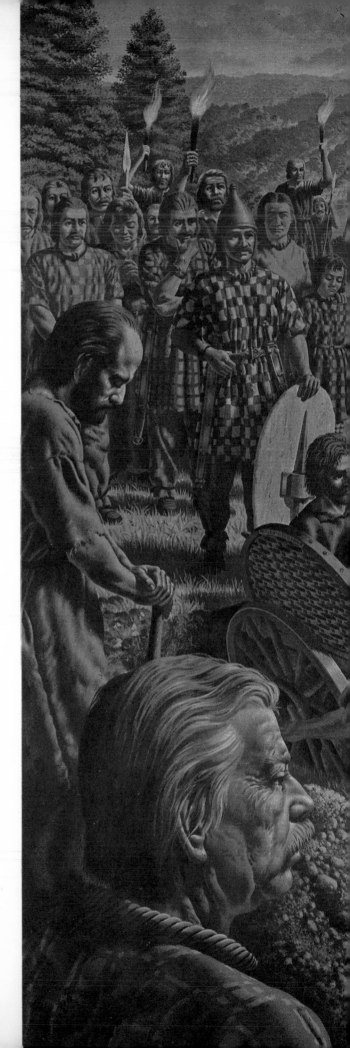

At a chieftain's funeral in the fifth century B.C., war chariot is lowered into the grave. Containers in foreground will be filled with food, which Celts believed the dead man would need in the afterworld.

Scythian warriors are depicted on the crest of a gold comb. This elaborate piece was found in a royal tomb.

The Druids also led the Celtic funeral ceremonies, which were elaborate affairs. Like many
other early peoples, the Celts believed that death
would give them the same pleasures they enjoyed
in life. When a man died, all the things he was
expected to need in the hereafter were buried with
him. As Druids prayed over the grave, a man's
weapons and jewelry, and vessels filled with food
and wine, were placed beside him. Tribal leaders
were buried in their full battle uniform, on their
chariots, and sometimes with their horses as well.

Because their tribal life was suited to movement

of unity may have permitted the Celtic tradition to last longer than it might have if they had been a closely knit nation. When the Romans, and later the Saxons, conquered their lands, small bands of Celts continued their way of life in the woods and wild fields of Scotland, Wales, and Ireland.

Despite a Roman occupation of Britain which lasted from A.D. 43 to about A.D. 400, the Celts held on to their own language and customs. When the Romans withdrew, the Saxons poured in, and remained for two hundred years. During this period the legend of King Arthur and his knights was started, and was kept alive in the years to come by the Celts. This was a time, too, when Christianity reached the Celts, especially those in Ireland. People of Celtic origin were still in Britain when it was invaded by the Danes, the Norse, and finally the Normans in 1066.

Even in France, where the Roman occupation was stricter than in Britain, the Celts retained their customs. In fact, some were imposed on their conquerors. The French language, although Latin in origin, is not what was spoken by the Romans. It was Latin as the Celts adapted it to their needs and style. Even important French place names reflect the Celtic period. Paris was the capital of the tribe of the Parisi, who had formed a town on

A Scythian warrior, portrayed on a vase, binds the wounds on a comrade's leg. The peaked hat, tied below chin, was part of the Scythian riding costume.

and temporary townships, and because they were so widely scattered, the Celts never formed a larger political system. As a result, there was no unity among them, and their society did not develop beyond a simple system of war chiefs as rulers and poor peasants as the lower classes. This very lack

Part of an equestrian neckpiece found in the Kuban region on the Black Sea. Fashioned of gold, and with blue enamel inlay, it is probably of Greek design.

Gold-plated plaque (below) used as belt decoration shows rider asleep in shade of tree. A companion holds the reins while the soldier's wife looks on.

an island in the Seine River. And the name of the river itself comes from the Sequani tribe.

The Scythians did not leave as rich a heritage as the Celts. When they were beaten by stronger bands of barbarians, they were swallowed up. But when the Scythians were the conquerors, and not the conquered, they made an impressive sight. On the march, looking for fresh pasture for their horses and cattle, they rode by the thousands. First came waves of cavalrymen on shaggy, fierce-looking animals. Behind them were mounted tribesmen driving huge herds of beasts, followed by ox-drawn wagons carrying wives, children, and household goods. In the rear limped the slaves.

Between 800 and 700 B.C., the Scythians were pushed from Asia by other tribes until they reached the shores of the Black Sea. They drove out the Cimmerians who lived there, and took over the rich land. Some Scythians settled down to become farmers. Others kept traveling, many as far west as Hungary, Romania, Bulgaria, and Prussia. Those who remained by the Black Sea became prosperous through trade. They supplied Greece with grain, salt, sturgeon, tuna, honey, meat, milk,

Detail from a felt-decorated cloth shows a mounted chief approaching throne of the Scythians' Great Goddess.

hides, furs, and most important, slaves. In return they received jewelry, metalwork, and fine pottery.

Since they were nomads, it is not surprising that Scythian life revolved around the horse. Much of their wealth was spent on bronze, silver, and gold ornaments, and jewelry for their horses. Handsomely worked eye-pieces and nose shields were fitted to the horse's head, and breastplates to the body. Pet horses were pampered and spoiled, and a Scythian's wealth was measured by the number of horses he owned. Like the Celts, the Scythians often buried horses with their dead masters. A tomb excavated in 1947 held the remains of nine horses, a wagon with a Chinese design, and a saddlecloth with Persian decoration.

The horse also brought about some changes in men's fashion. Instead of skirts or robes of skin, trousers were invented. This item of clothing, so practical to horsemen, first appeared among the Scythians. The first Europeans to wear trousers were the Celts, who may have learned about them in one of their meetings with the Scythians.

Wood carving shows a dragon devouring an elk head. Much Scythian art depicts animals in frenzied motion.

Horses were not the only animals to have an influence on Scythian life. As hunters, the Scythians came to know the wild beasts and birds of prey. In the Altai Mountains of Asia they were confronted with lions, leopards, elk, buffalo, wolves, bears, eagles, and vultures. In European Russia they hunted milder animals such as mink, beaver, and otter. And on the plains below the mountain range which covered Siberia, Mongolia, and Turkestan, they chased wild horses to add to their collections.

These animals appear prominently in Scythian art. With great skill, animal figures were formed in bronze, gold, wood, leather, and felt. Sword hilts were topped with animal heads. Vases and pitchers often had handles shaped like animal bodies. Trousers, boots, and rugs were embroidered with animal figures. Most of the time these figures were realistic. Occasionally, the Scythians used fantastic animals such as the dragon and the griffin, which they borrowed from Chinese or Persian art.

One of the most important elements in the Scythian animal art was the use of antlers. They were often elaborate or exaggerated in shape or form. The special importance of antlers may have come from earlier Eurasian nomads who attached a religious meaning to them. It is possible that they thought the stag was the animal which carried the souls of the dead to the world beyond. Stags are often depicted on Scythian funeral objects, and masks topped by antlers were often placed on horses buried with their masters. This may have been done to give the horse the swiftness of the stag, and thus speed the journey of the dead.

Despite their wealth, their mastery of the horse, and their military skills, the Scythians did not survive as a nation. At one time they had held Darius, the Persian, at bay, and a hundred years later they resisted Philip of Macedon. But by 100 B.C. they disappeared from history. The reasons for this are mainly geographical. The Scythians had no natural barrier against invasion. Their great plains were open, and the Volga and Danube Rivers were easily crossed. Even more important, these rich grasslands were tempting to other nomads.

The Scythians were thus constantly being pushed back by people from central Asia, but their immediate conquerors were the Sarmatians. Like the Scythians, the Sarmatians were superb horsemen, and they had developed some improvements for battle, including the metal stirrup. The Scythian townships fell quickly to the Sarmatians. The Scythians could not move west because that way was blocked by Germanic tribes. As they were driven eastward their numbers grew smaller, until at last they vanished.

The Scythian tradition did not disappear with them, however. The Sarmatians passed part of it on to the Alans, another tribe. The Alans passed it on to the Khazar empire, which flourished in Russia between A.D. 750 and A.D. 1000. The Khazar empire controlled the trade route between Byzantium—present-day Istanbul—and Sweden. When this hold was broken by the Slavs and the Norse, and the road was opened to all people, missionaries as well as traders started to use it. Over this road, Christianity was brought to the Slavs, the last of the European peoples to emerge from barbarism to civilization.

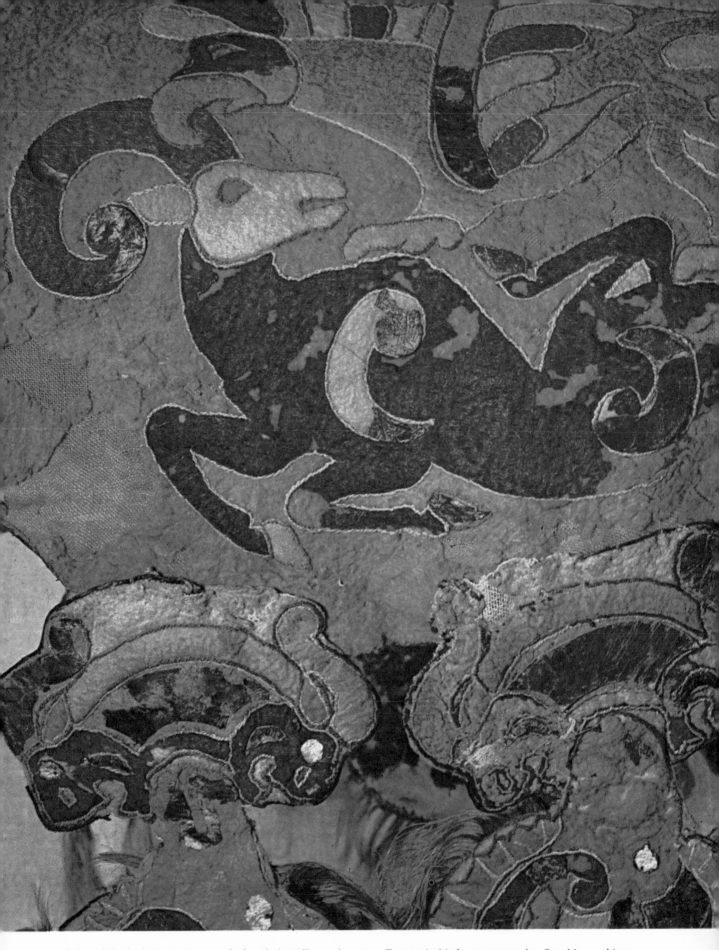

A felt saddlecloth depicts an eagle-headed griffin and a ram. Fantastic birds were popular Scythian subjects.

Shang memorial mask, designed to hang on a wall, shows resemblance of these ancient people to modern Chinese.

108

CHAPTER 11

THE SHANG
Men Who Made China

Civilization did not come to eastern Asia until some 1,500 years after it had flourished in the Middle East. When it did, it produced a way of life as rich as that which was known to the Egyptians. What is more, the first known civilization of Asia may have left a greater mark on the generations which followed it than did some of the better known ones in the Middle East. The bases for the modern civilizations of China, Japan, and other parts of the Far East can be found in an ancient one which lasted for six hundred years on the plains of North China.

From roughly 1700 to 1100 B.C., a group of people we call the Shang lived in dozens of cities and towns on the rich Yellow River plain. Around them were the primitive villages of peasants who still lived as they did in the Stone Age. But in the Shang cities, artisans worked marble, jade, ivory, bone, and bronze, and wove fine silks. Handwriting, the ancestor of modern Chinese writing, had been developed, and a complicated form of religion had come into being.

The rise of the Shang in the midst of a barbarous land is one of the mysteries in the story of man. The Shangs' ways of building and farming, of growing silk, and even some aspects of their religion, could have come from the Neolithic culture around them. But this could not have been true of the complex system of writing, of working bronze, of horse-drawn chariots, or of elaborate funerals, all of which the Shang introduced to Asia. There

is little real evidence that these accomplishments came from the earlier civilizations of the Middle East. But scholars assume that they must have originated there, and in ways we do not yet know, traveled the long distance from west to east.

However the skills of civilization reached them, the Shangs used them with imagination and vigor. They were a robust people who enjoyed war for

Bronze helmet has a socket for an ornamental feather.

109

Wind instrument above, used by the Shang in social festivities and religious rites, is 2.2 inches long.

sport as well as for victory, who hunted and held lavish banquets. Men and women dressed in furs and fine silk fabrics. They wore jewelry made of bone, shell, and jade, and had elaborate hairdos which they kept in place by long ivory and bone hairpins.

Shang society was divided into at least two classes—the warrior nobility and the peasants. The government was headed by the *wang,* or king, who made all important decisions. Under him were about twenty titled officials who had military, civil, and secretarial duties. The most important of these were the *yin.* They were responsible for the management of the royal household, feasts, and agriculture. The *tso-ts'e* kept the court records, the *shih* priests were in charge of sacrifices, and the *kung* provided the king's music.

While the lower classes followed primitive ways, the court nobility indulged in a life of pleasure. Hunting was a favorite sport. Large expeditions

Bizarre bird at right, called a k'uei-feng, *decorates a sacrificial caldron. The huge vessels, often three feet high, held meat offerings to royal ancestors.*

110

Tripod cup, or chüeh, *has a water buffalo on handle. Almost 11 inches high, it was used for millet wine.*

to distant hunting grounds were often organized. Sometimes live animals were captured and displayed in the royal zoo. One record of the time says, "Hunting on this day, we actually captured one tiger, 40 deer, 164 foxes, 159 hornless deer...."

Closely allied to hunting was warfare. Weaker neighbors called the Shang "the great terror of the east." Kings probably kept a small standing army, but could raise a large one on short notice. For a small raiding expedition they would lead a thousand men, for larger battles as many as thirty thousand. Warfare was almost perpetual for the Shangs since they continually tried to subdue the barbaric people surrounding them—"the people in the four directions all around," as one scribe wrote.

Their military force was highly organized. Shang documents indicate that special officials were put in charge of horses, dogs, and archery. In close combat, the Shang used a weapon called the *ko,* or dagger-ax, a pointed, double-edged blade on a wooden shaft. For long-range fighting, the most important weapon was a bow which shot arrows of bronze, stone, or bone. The Shang also used horse-drawn chariots with great effectiveness. The vehicles had two huge wheels nearly five feet in diameter, and were pulled by two or four horses. It is likely that the chariots were manned to defend the commanding officer in the field. There is also an instance of the Shangs using an elephant in battle against the eastern barbarians.

The peaceful pursuits of the Shang were expressed in beautiful carvings. Their work in bronze is ranked among the finest metalwork ever created by man. Bronze vessels were cast in a rich variety of shapes and sizes. No two vessels have been found to be exactly alike. Their surfaces were decorated with complicated designs and a vast assortment of animals—wild and domestic, real and imaginary. The most farfetched animals were created by mixing the body of one with the head of a second, the tail of a third, and the legs of a fourth. Scholars are not sure why the Shang created these monsters, but believe they may have some religious meaning.

Animals were also a favorite subject for stone sculpture. Many were carved from a soft, white marble called *ta li shih,* others from jade, which is still a favorite stone of Chinese craftsmen today. Jade was quite difficult to work. It was also expensive, because it had to be imported from Chinese

Bronze and turquoise ornaments, designed for horses and chariots, were often buried with their owners.

Turkestan, some 2,000 miles away, or from Lake Baikal, Siberia, 1,000 miles away. Most of the sculpture was small, but recent excavations have uncovered an oxhead larger than life size.

Aside from animals, the best known design of Shang artistry is the so-called *t'ao-t'eh,* a mask composed of right and left profiles facing each other and joined to form a grotesque face. As with the animals, scholars believe that this design may have had some special religious or magical meaning.

However large a part these bronze and stone objects played in the religious life of the Shang, they were certainly important in time of death. Some of the largest bronze vessels and jade and marble carvings have been found in the tombs of Shang kings. Alongside them were fine silks and pottery, great stores of elaborately carved weapons, and enough musical instruments for an entire orchestra.

The vast riches which were buried with kings were only one aspect of elaborate, and often grisly, funerals. Enormous holes in the shape of inverted pyramids were dug into the earth by hand. One tomb was sixty feet square and forty-three feet deep. The main entrance was a sloping ramp facing south, often as long as 150 feet. Entrances in the other three directions were steeper and shorter. The main pit was carefully leveled, after which a *yao-k'eng,* or small "waist pit," was dug. This was used to bury a dog or a watchman to guard the dead king. In one tomb there were nine such small pits, each with the remains of a dog and a kneeling human guard holding a jade or bronze dagger-ax.

Above the small pits, the Shang built a coffin chamber out of thick planks of cypress. The walls were smoothed with white lime and decorated with red paint and inlays of boar tusks. The empty space between the coffin chamber and the pit walls was then refilled with soil which was stamped down tightly to provide a flat shelf. The offerings of metal and stone work, fabrics, weapons, and instruments were placed on the earthen shelf

At a royal burial, in a huge underground pit, human victim is about to be beheaded by executioner (lower left) while other victims wait on passageway steps.

At a banquet, perhaps celebrating a successful hunt, Shang lords and ladies dine on assorted meats and strong millet wine. The diners, here laughing at a joke told by their host (center rear), kneel on rush matting and eat with chopsticks, as the Chinese still do. A small orchestra provides music for the guests who dine from fine pottery, ivory, and bronze. The mural on the wall was suggested by paintings found in Shang tombs.

within the wooden coffin chamber and in the four passageways. Once a ruler's zoo, including monkeys, birds, and an elephant, were put in the burial chamber. The treasures in place, the burial pit was then filled.

Nearly all royal burials were accompanied by human sacrifice, sometimes on a large scale. It is believed that the Shang may have looked on the mass slaughter as a way to provide the dead king with slaves in the after-life, or to appease the gods. The victims, who were decapitated in groups, were probably slaves or prisoners of war. Often their heads were buried separately from their bodies.

As with other early people, the Shang had many gods. One reason for this was that dead kings were given the status of gods. For the most part, the Shang religion revolved around ancestor worship, which is still widely practiced in China. In addition, the Shang had gods of the wind, the clouds, the sun, the moon, and the hills. The most powerful of these was Shang Ti, the Ruler Above, who had power over the weather, farming, and war. Christian missionaries today use Shang Ti as the word to translate the name of God in China.

The Shang sought to learn the future from the spirits of their dead ancestors. A special class of diviners called *shen-jen* interpreted the answers. Questions were written on the shells of tortoises or on the shoulder blades of oxen. Because the Latin word for shoulder blade is scapula, scholars have applied the word "scapulimancy" to this method of seeking to know the future. The diviners applied heat to the shell or bone, which caused cracks to appear. The size, shape, and direction of the cracks were the basis for the answers.

Scapulimancy was used by the Shang kings for a wide variety of purposes. They often asked about forthcoming weather, the prospects for a hunting trip or a battle. Sometimes they were very personal. "When will the crown prince recover from his illness?" and "Will the queen bear me a son or daughter?" are examples of some of the questions that have been found. One king wanted to learn which of his ancestors had been responsible for his toothache.

Most of what we know about the Shang has come from the writings on these bones and on other materials. More than 100,000 bones and shells have been dug up in the fields of North China. In addition, studies have been made of the writings on bronze, pottery, even hairpins, and, in one case, a human skull. This one described the sacrifice of the chief of a Shang tribe to his ancestor king. The Shang used about three thousand different characters in their writing. So far, only a third have been deciphered, and some three hundred scholars continue to work on the problem. Their efforts are called chiakuology, from the Chinese *chia-ku-hsüeh,* which means the study of bone and shell writings.

The Shang writing, although the earliest Chinese writing we know, was well developed. It had probably started centuries earlier as simple pictographs similar to those of the Middle East. But so far we have no evidence of the changes which the Shang made, or how and when they took place. Modern Chinese writing, which still uses pictographs to represent things, and ideographs to represent ideas, is directly descended from the Shang. Most of the ways in which Chinese characters are now formed—to show pronunciation and meaning—were used by the Shang.

The Shang left modern Asia more than a way of writing. Although they were conquered sometime in the twelfth or eleventh century B.C. by a people called the Chou, their way of life persisted. The Chou, who came out of the western highlands, were led by Wou Wang, who is called the Martial King. He invaded Shang territory with 50,000 men and could not be stopped. The last of the Shang kings, facing defeat, fled to his palace, dressed himself in fine clothes and jewelry, and killed himself by throwing himself into the flames of the burning palace.

The Chou were not as advanced as the Shang, but they soon absorbed all the skills of the defeated enemy. They took over many of the Shang ideas in law and religion, and in time improved on the Shang system of government. They continued the Shang art of writing, and their artistic accomplishments as well.

The Chou Dynasty is divided by historians into two major periods. The Western Chou, whose capital was on the Wei River near modern Siam, were defeated by barbarians about 770 B.C. The

Contours of jade elephant follow shape of the stone.

capital was moved to Loyang, two hundred miles to the east, where the Eastern Chou period started. It did not last long, however. Its importance declined during a period of constant warfare between 481 B.C. and 221 B.C. Out of the numerous struggles which took place, several separate states were formed in China. Finally, the state of Ch'in emerged as the strongest. It swallowed up its rivals, wrote one historian, as "a silkworm devours a mulberry leaf."

Limestone frog and turtle are simple and realistic.

The state of Ch'in, which gave its name to modern China, united the country for the first time as a great empire. The Great Wall of China goes back to this period. From the Chinese heartland a great civilization developed. It penetrated a vast territory from Inner Mongolia to Vietnam, from Tibet to Japan. Chinese farmers not only carried with them their skills—especially in rice growing—but the Chinese culture as well. Their influence was felt most strongly in Korea, Japan, and Vietnam.

From Korea, which was at various times part of the Chinese state, Japan borrowed major parts of the Chinese civilization. Japanese writing, diet, clothing, art, and literature have their origins in ancient China. The Japanese even inherited the practice of kneeling on the floor, and maintained it long after the Chinese took to chairs. For a thousand years Japan and Korea were dominated by the Chinese civilization. Gradually these countries went their separate, although still related, ways.

"Korean culture and experience seem like variations on Chinese themes," a scholar has written. "Japanese culture and experience show what very different tunes can be played with the same set of instruments." He could have added that the instruments were shaped by the Shang, the remarkably creative ancestors of Chinese civilization.

Monster with sharp fangs and jagged teeth has the head of a tiger and the body of a semi-human creature. It is made of white marble, one of the many materials used by Shang craftsmen to create finely sculpted objects.

CHAPTER 12

MAYA AND AZTEC
Men of the New World

The Americas—North, Middle, and South— are sometimes called the New World. The only reason for this, of course, is that these continents were "new" to European explorers and map-makers. Actually, they are as old as the Old World, and the civilizations which rose on their land have made contributions comparable to those of the early civilizations on the shores of the Mediterranean.

Scholars are now convinced that men crossed from Asia to America during the last Ice Age when the Bering Strait was a solid mass. Seeking game to hunt, they traveled southward across the Americas. Man-made flake tools going back 24,000 years have been discovered at the Tule Springs, Nevada. Remains of campsites more than 10,000 years old have been found near the Strait of Magellan.

Archaeologists are still tracing the mysteries of man's development in the New World, and theories are constantly being changed. Pottery dating back to 1500 B.C. has been found in Middle America. More importantly, it is of such fine quality that scholars feel that there must have been many years

Wall painting at left, from the eighth century Maya temple city of Bonampak, shows high priest robed in jaguar skin, jade ornaments, and plumed headdress.

of development before such work could have been achieved. It is likely that a great many cultures were advancing separately at the same time in villages from El Salvador in the south to the valley of central Mexico in the north. By 2000 B.C. these people had turned from hunting to the cultivation of corn, or maize, which is a native American plant. With farming as a base, villages came into being. Eventually, these villages grew into larger societies.

Of these early American civilizations, an outstanding one was that of the Maya, who flourished in the jungles of Guatemala and the Yucatán peninsula of Mexico. The beginnings of the Maya, like those of the cultures which rose with them, are still largely unclear. We know that around the third century A.D. they were already an advanced people. By then they were building great temples and pyramids of stone and mortar, and adorning them with fine sculpture and wall paintings. They had evolved a system of pictograph writing, which unfortunately has not yet been completely deciphered. They had created a calendar more accurate than any in use in Europe at the time, and they had studied astronomy.

The people who reached this advanced state led lives dominated almost completely by their own form of religion. It had developed from a

119

Tikal temple, seen before archaeologists dug it out.

Maya man in pottery wears typically large jewelry.

primitive worship of jungle animals until it reached the stars and time itself. Priest-astronomers studied the skies and consulted calendar tables. The answers they found became clues for Maya behavior. The people acted only in accordance with what was foretold for each day.

But this religion allowed some leeway to the Maya. If one set of gods was not considered favorable, it was discarded for a new one. Certain gods reigned for a year or more, others for as little as a week or a day. The priests encouraged this. Their main concern was to guide the people on how to get around the gods. They would counsel tribes, families, or individuals on when to sell corn and when to marry. It is thought likely that during this period in Maya life, the priests were the rulers of the people as well, and that under them there were many years of peace.

Religion was not only a private affair for the Maya, but a public affair as well. They probably spent a third of their time at public religious ceremonies. These were usually held at tremendous shrines, like the Great Plaza of Tikal, a holy city overlooking the Guatemalan jungle. All the Maya skills in art and architecture were reflected in these temples. Beautiful stone friezes decorated the temple roofs, pillars were finely carved, and clay and jade were sculpted into handsome objects.

During this period in Maya history, there were only occasional lapses from worship or the arts associated with it. An interesting one, however, was a ball game which seems to resemble soccer. It is called *pok-ta-pok* in Maya. During the game a solid rubber ball about the size of a volleyball was knocked around an area about as big as a basketball court. The ball was advanced by bumping it with hip, elbow, or wrist. It must have produced quite a bit of excitement, as well as a number of injuries. Carvings of the time show players padded at elbows, knees, chest, and backsides.

The Maya continued to produce sculptured monuments and fine art until about A.D. 900. Then, for reasons which are still a mystery, the Maya civilization began to fade, and the beautiful ceremonial cities in the south eventually became deserted.

The Maya did not die out, however. They reappeared in the Yucatán peninsula to the north, but with many changes. The warlike Toltecs, who rose to power in the Valley of Mexico and moved south to the Yucatán peninsula, subjugated some of the Maya and influenced the rest.

The Toltecs had their own god, Quetzalcoatl, who was known as Kukulkán in Yucatán, and a favorite ornament, the feathered serpent. With the coming of the Toltecs, the Maya sculpture and carvings became more warlike. At about this time, too, the Maya were putting heavy emphasis on human sacrifice in their religion. During famines or drought, living victims, preferably children, were thrown into a 130-foot-deep "Well of Sacrifice." This new religion held that the sun, which was the source of energy, had to be fed after a night of sleep. Wars were fought to find prisoners to feed the sun.

Long before the Spanish conquerors arrived in Mexico in 1527, the greatest of the Maya buildings had been abandoned. What was once a unified people became small city-states at constant warfare with each other. Scholars are hard put to explain the decline. They have suggested the possibility of changes in the climate, exhaustion of the soil, disease, revolution, or the rulers' sudden inability to govern.

Neither is it known why three other cultures which rose in Mexico also grew and then faded. Though they differed from the Maya in speech, local customs, and artistic skills and style, the others shared many of the same attributes. The Teotihuacán built majestic monuments in the Valley of Mexico, the 2,000-year-old pyramids of the Sun and the Moon. The Olmecs in the lowland regions of Veracruz and Tabasco were master carvers of stone, especially jade. Some Olmec monuments are believed to be older than those of the earliest Maya. The Zapotecs and Mixtecs of Oaxaca built lavish tombs 2,500 years ago.

The last of the great civilizations to emerge in the Valley of Mexico was the Aztec. Its people were descended from small, nomadic tribes from the north of the valley. They fought their way

A time marker shows the elaborate hieroglyphics on the back of a stela, or stone monument. The pillar marked passage of five-, ten-, and twenty-year periods.

south and made homes on an island in Lake Texcoco. The god of these warriors, called Huitzilopochtli, had to be fed human blood to live. Long before the Spanish landed, the Aztecs had conquered most of Mexico and had begun to shape its future.

The Aztecs had learned to live and worship by the calendar, as had the Maya and others before them. But they gave themselves over to their religion with a greater passion than any of their predecessors. In elaborate ceremonies fixed by the sacred calendar, human sacrifice was always the final act. Often, still-beating hearts were removed from the bodies of victims not yet dead. Long racks of skulls adorned the temple squares in the main Aztec cities and towns. At one festival it was reported that 20,000 captives were slaughtered on the high altar.

It is not strange, therefore, to find that death was the basis for all Aztec thinking. In their sculptures of the gods, Aztec artists expressed the Aztec vision of death. The temples were conceived around the altar, where the sacrifices were held. The calendar itself was proof to the Aztecs that each day's life was a favor of the gods. "The Aztec," said a Mexican archaeologist, "stamps the horror of death on all of his creations."

Neither this constant association with death nor a reputation as great warriors could prepare the

Feathered serpent, at the base of a column guarding a sacred portal at Chichén Itzá, is the emblem of Quetzalcoatl, to whom pyramid temple is dedicated.

Aztecs for their own final defeat. They had subdued most of the countryside around them and had ruled from a tremendous city. Tenochtitlán, a lake-city of some 60,000 families, was probably the biggest capital city in the Americas before 1840. But not even this was enough to stop the advance of the Spaniards' horses and cannon.

The Aztecs had been warned about the coming of strangers. Montezuma the Younger, Emperor of the Aztecs, had received signs from his priests. But all the omens pointed to the return from the east of Quetzalcoatl, the bearded, white-skinned god of all Mexicans. A temple had caught fire, a comet had been seen by day, and Montezuma himself had seen a host of armed men in his mirror. Then, in 1519, a watchman came to Montezuma. "Lord and king of ours," he said, "forgive my daring. I walked to the seashore and I saw a kind of mountain or big hill moving about in the sea without touching the shore."

That was how Montezuma learned that Hernando Cortes had arrived with eleven ships, some five hundred men, sixteen horses, and ten cannon. Cortes had already been to Tabasco, where he quickly perceived that the Indians thought his

Temple of the Warriors at Chichén Itzá stands on the summit of a pyramid. The terraces are typically Toltec.

musketeers were gods with lightning in their hands, and that his horsemen were four-legged monsters with human bodies. He sailed to a point near Veracruz, where he was met by noblemen acting as messengers for Montezuma. They offered Cortes a helmet filled with gold dust and other valuable gifts, and asked him to leave. But Cortes decided to march against Montezuma.

Cortes scuttled his ships as a sign that there would be no retreat and led his men over great mountain passes into the land of the Tlaxcalans. These people hated the Aztecs and welcomed the support of Cortes in defeating them. With his own small force and 1,000 Tlaxcalans, Cortes entered the Aztec capital. He struck violently, destroying throne and temple. He held Montezuma hostage, burned some of his ministers alive, and ordered that gold be brought as tribute. For three days the

The Pyramid of the Sun, just north of Mexico City, monument of the 2,000-year-old city of Teotihuacán, was built by the spare-time labor of 10,000 peasants.

crossed the causeway which bridged the lake, many of them fell into the water. Because of the weight of the gold they carried they were dragged under and quickly drowned. During that retreat, which the Spanish call *la noche triste,* the sad night, Cortes lost three-fourths of his men.

Despite heavy onslaughts by the aroused Aztecs, Cortes made his way to his allies in Tlaxcala. There he regrouped his forces and marched on Tenochtitlán again. The Aztecs, under the leadership of Cuauhtémoc, Montezuma's nephew and son-in-law, fought furiously. Battles raged on the streets, the causeways, and in boats on the lake itself. Cortes was nearly captured at one point. Many of his soldiers were seized, and immediately dragged to the altar and killed. Despite their losses, the Spanish and their allies pushed on, sometimes counting their gains in inches and feet.

At last, with food running low, the Aztecs gave up. Cuauhtémoc tried to escape in a canoe, but was captured. When he was brought before Cortes,

The Plumed Serpent of Quetzalcoatl (below) is visible throughout Mexico. This is a fifth century example.

Aztec goldsmiths melted their beautiful ornaments into gold bars that were equal in value to more than $6,000,000.

Had Cortes stopped there he might have left safely with this fortune. But at that point he smashed the idols of Tenochtitlán, and the Aztecs rose in revenge. When Montezuma tried to keep the people calm, they stoned him to death. The Spaniards were forced to flee the city. As they

Ceremonial shield of feathers carries symbolic head.

he said, "I have done all that I could to defend myself and my people." Then, pointing to a dagger, he said, "Better dispatch me with this and rid me of my life at once." But Cortes had other uses for the Aztec ruler. He kept him as hostage for three years to make sure there would be no further uprising. At the end of that time Cortes ordered Cuauhtémoc hanged.

The emperor's death was the symbol of the passing of the Aztec civilization. From that time on Spanish speech, religion, and government were imposed on what had been his realm. But today, after four centuries, the Indian population has not been wiped out in Mexico. One-third of the people are pure-blooded Indians, descended from the Aztecs and the Maya who preceded them. Cuauhtémoc is considered a national hero; Cortes is remembered as a villain.

Before they were conquered by the invaders from the Old World, the civilizations of Middle America had an effect that carried beyond their own borders. They influenced the Indian tribes who lived north of them in areas that are now part of the United States. Their influence was strongest among the Indian groups nearest them—those not far from the Rio Grande River. It did not reach to the Great Plains and Canada, where the Indians remained nomadic hunters and warriors until they were subdued by the white men.

More than 1,500 years ago, the Basket Maker Indians of the American Southwest were living in village societies much like those which had appeared in Middle America hundreds of years earlier. Their crops included maize and beans, which had been developed first in Middle America. At sites in southern Arizona, archaeologists have found ball courts which resemble those used in the Yucatán peninsula and central Mexico. In the fifteenth century A.D. people in the lower Mississippi Valley were building pyramidal mounds with temples on top. These were similar to those built by the Maya. One produced by the Mound Builders, called Emerald Mound, is thirty-five feet high and covers seven acres.

The Pueblo Indians of the Southwest were also maize farmers, and led settled lives similar to those of the Indians of Mexico. Instead of worshiping at mounds, however, the Pueblos dug holes in the ground for their religious rites. Oraibi, a Hopi Pueblo village in Arizona, goes back to A.D. 1150 and may be the oldest continuously inhabited place in the United States. Other cliff colonies, built more than 850 years ago as a defense against the invading Navajo, have been abandoned. The Navajo stole sheep from the Spaniards to provide themselves with food and clothing, and settled down to become shepherds. Today they are the most numerous of all Indian tribes in the United States.

The Plains Indians to the north also gained from the Spaniards, but in a way which was to keep them from ever settling down. They captured lost Spanish horses, and later stole others. They soon became outstanding horsemen, a skill which gave fresh meaning to their nomadic lives. The

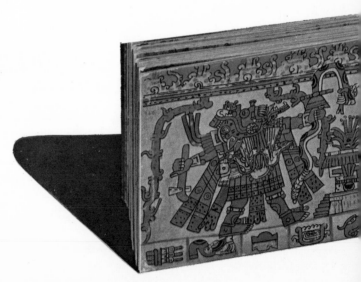

Figures from western Mexico depict home life with lively realism. One plays a drum, one holds a child, one holds a plate. They wear rings in their noses, ornaments on their ears, and bangles on their arms. The Aztecs knew how to work and cast metals, and did so for decorative purposes like this, but rarely for practical uses.

A codex, or graphic historical record, is unfolded to show four rain gods perhaps revered by the Mixtecs, who lived at the same time as the Aztecs. The hieroglyphics along the bottom of the pages mark days of the calendar.

Gold ornament, perhaps worn on an Aztec warrior's chest, represents a man with the jaws of a jaguar.

The long-tongued serpent with golden fangs is a lip ornament. It fits into a slit in wearer's lower lip.

Dakota, Cheyenne, Pawnee, Sioux, and Comanche fought each other, and eventually the white men, on horseback. As buffalo hunting became easier, the Plains tribes followed the wandering herds in treks extending hundreds of miles. These are the Indians most people know best from books, movies, and television.

In California, and north to Puget Sound, the Indians lived in settled communities. But they were fishermen instead of farmers. Shellfish was the staple in California, although some of the tribes also ground flour from acorns. To the north, salmon, seals, and whales supported the population. In these areas, artistic and religious forms were carved and painted on totem poles and smaller wood pieces.

In the American Southeast, the most advanced tribes were the Creeks, Cherokees, and Natchez. The Creeks and Cherokees were farmers. They lived in villages built of houses made from the barks of trees. The Natchez, who may have been descended from the Mound Builders, were ruled by a person known as "the Sun." He was dressed in an elaborate feathered coat which resembled Aztec dress.

North of the Natchez lived the Iroquois, who were joined in a league called the Five Nations. This was probably the most advanced political organization north of Middle America. Of these tribes, the Mohawks were chosen as the warriors. They raided surrounding tribes, usually the Algonquins. The Algonquins were also being pushed back by the European settlers on the Atlantic coast. Between the Iroquois and the colonists, the Algonquins were reduced to helplessness.

At their peak, the Indians who lived in what is now the United States and Canada numbered about 900,000. They were split up among 350 different tribes, each with a different language. Few of them made any effort to learn the language of another, and when they met they resorted to sign language, one of their most important inventions. As recently as 1900 it was believed that they were on their way to extinction. By the Census of 1960, however, there were 523,591 Indians in the United States alone, and their numbers are growing. They are now in no more danger of being wiped out than those of Middle America.

Aztec ceremonial mask is made of cedarwood with mosaics of turquoise. Eye holes are for wearer to see through.

CHAPTER 13

THE INCA
Men of the Mountains

Throughout the world, the growth of a civilization started when men settled down to work the land instead of hunting for their food. That they did this in the rich valleys blessed by good climate is not surprising. The lands around the Nile, the Tigris-Euphrates, and the Indus were amazingly bountiful.

Special notice must therefore be taken of those people who created an advanced way of life where nature was not so generous. Perhaps no group did so much with so little as those who lived 11,000 feet above sea level on the Andes Mountains of Peru.

Far to the south of the Aztecs and Maya, the Andeans created a civilization in some of the world's most forbidding terrain. By irrigating and terracing the mountainsides, they managed to raise fine crops. Many of their plants were completely unknown to the Old World: the potato, tomato, yam, and lima bean. They cultivated cotton, and tamed the llama and alpaca for their fine wool. By the time corn was introduced from Middle America about 900 B.C., the farmers of South America were among the best in the world.

Starting about 1200 B.C., the Andean civilization passed through six distinct stages. The last of these, the Inca empire, was a remarkably unified state. The achievements of the Inca were as remarkable as those of the Romans. They built big

cities, irrigation works, and vast highways. They organized the arts of weaving and pottery making. Their suspension bridges, tunnels, and fortresses are monuments to superb engineering. Yet this amazing empire high on the Andes could not have been possible without the contributions of the people who preceded it. It was, in fact, a logical extension of the cultures which the earlier Andean peoples established.

The first of these is called the Chavín, for Chavín de Huántar, a 2,800-year-old ruin in the remote northern highlands of Peru. The Chavín lasted until about 400 B.C., and appear to have been as absorbed in their religion as the Maya. Their temples are considered by some experts to be even finer than those of the later Inca. The one at Chavín is a massive, three-story stone building, 246 feet square. It is surrounded by pyramidal platforms, paved terraces, and plazas. Within is a honeycomb of passages and a special system of ventilating shafts.

The most impressive features of Chavín are the stone sculptures and carved slabs that are set into its smooth walls. Whether the figures are men, animals, or birds, they have a feline mouth akin

A nobleman's portrait adorns the 1,700-year-old jar at right. This jar, which probably dates back to the Mochica culture, was found on north coast of Peru.

131

to that of a puma, jaguar, or cat. On one monster this mouth appears at twelve different places on the body. It glares from the head and tail of a snake. The best guess is that it was a symbol for some supernatural power. Putting it on men and other creatures may have served to make them supernatural.

Chavin has raised other mysteries. No graves have been found there, which would indicate that people may not have lived there continuously. The careful construction of the temple supports the theory that it was a religious center. Perhaps people from nearby came on pilgrimages at certain seasons of the year. At these times they may have worked together to drag stones into place. When this was completed, artisans may have done the carving and other fine work. But however this was accomplished, the influence of the feline art at Chavín has remained in Peru until the present day.

Starting about 400 B.C. another culture began to form in the river valleys south of what is now the city of Lima. Modern scholars call this group Paracas, after the modern name of the peninsula on which some of its burial vaults have been found.

The Paracas, as far as we know, did not build any large buildings. Ancestor worship seems to have been the major theme of their religion. Almost all the findings from Paracas indicate a great respect for the dead.

Wonderful clothes, whose colors still glow after 2,200 years, have been found in the Paracas tombs. Some of the weaving was of such fineness that it contained up to five hundred threads per square inch. Many of the mantles for the dead were painted with the feline features found in Chavín art. Others were embroidered with strange figures —winged men with snakes coiled around their eyes, split-headed condors gobbling fish, and cat-faced men with knives.

It is probable that entire communities worked together to make the clothes for the dead. Rich mantles, copper battle-axes, and gold ornaments

Machu Picchu, a fortress city built on many levels, straddles a mountain ridge 8,000 feet above the sea. Agricultural terraces were built outside the city.

were buried with some people, who may have been warriors or priests. Yet these people were found side by side with others who were buried more modestly. Scholars think this means there were no class distinctions among the Paracas, as there were to be later among other Andean peoples.

In the third Andean period, beginning about A.D. 400, the Nazca succeeded the Paracas in the south, while the Mochica rose in the north. The Mochica subdued their neighbors and evolved a complicated society. They laid roads and began to make pottery, skills which the later Inca were to take over. It seems likely that the Mochica were able to accomplish what they did by employing large groups of workers, directed by a small group of leaders.

Under such a system it was possible for the Mochica to build the Pyramid of the Sun, which is

This 2,500-year-old jug is shaped as a seated girl.

the biggest monument found on the Peruvian coast. It contains 130 million adobe bricks. Further evidence of this class system is found in their painted pottery, much of which shows bejeweled chieftains carried on litters, or banquets in which the chiefs dine at the head table. Aside from depicting life among the leaders, Mochica pottery reflects what must have been the daily lives of ordinary citizens—fighting, farming, fishing, and hunting.

We do not know how long the Mochica culture lasted, but about A.D. 1000 another group made itself felt in the southern Andes, and throughout most of Peru. These people built a vast ceremonial center at Tiahuanaco on the plains south of Lake Titicaca. This body of water is 12,506 feet above sea level and is the highest navigable lake in the world. Stone buildings and giant statues dot the plain. One is an unfinished pyramid whose ground plan is slightly smaller than that of the Great Pyramid of Egypt. A ten-foot doorway called the Gateway to the Sun, now restored by scholars, is decorated with a handsome frieze. It shows a god-like figure surrounded by numbers of small puma heads and patterned figures of winged men bearing weapons.

Tiahuanaco is so bleak that chances are it was not a center of population, but a ceremonial spot. Scholars lean to the theory that it served much the same purpose as Chavín de Huántar to the north. It is likely, too, that its beautiful buildings were constructed by groups of pilgrims.

Until the Tiahuanaco period, no single culture dominated all of Peru. The high mountains and the vast deserts had probably made it impossible. But somehow the people of Tiahuanaco accomplished what previous cultures had not. The designs found at the Tiahuanaco ceremonial center are repeated on ceramics, wood, and metal made throughout Peru at about the same time. No one knows how the Tiahuanaco expansion took place. There is no evidence that it came entirely through military conquest, which was the way such influence was often spread elsewhere. But however it

A cat man holding a human trophy head (left) is on a fragment of mantle which the ancestor worshipers of Paracas wove for their dead some 2,000 years ago.

was accomplished, it prepared the way for the final stages of Andean civilization.

The fifth period brought the Chimu people of the north to the fore. We know very little about them except that they were the immediate fore-runners of the Inca, the last of the Andean civilizations. Out of the Inca talent for organization an empire was created from the series of cultures which had risen and died in the Andes.

The Inca divided their 5,000,000 subjects into "the land of the four quarters," each ruled by a nobleman. They also divided their capital city of Cuzco into four quarters to correspond with those established in the country, and visitors had to stay in their appropriate section. After a nation-wide

Wide-eyed fisherman and nets adorn a Nazca clay jar.

135

census, the Inca emperor then appointed officials who were responsible at various levels. The highest was placed over 10,000 men, the next over 1,000, the next over 500, down to leaders appointed to supervise as few as fifty and ten men. All but the last two officials were nobles, and each was responsible to the one above him. Messengers raced over the emperor's paved roads carrying reports from lower officials to the ones above them.

Under such a division, a rigid class system was inescapable. Workers had to contribute work or goods to the state, which ran all the factories for making cloth, ceramics, and gold jewelry. These objects were for the nobility or for ceremonial use. In most of the towns and along the highways were state-owned warehouses, which the people had to keep filled in case of shortage or a requisition from the emperor. Conquered peoples were required to pay tribute. The Inca had even worked out a way for keeping track of these taxes, by a system of tying knots in a set of colored strings called the *quipu*.

Graceful beaker of Tiahuanaco uses puma decoration.

The Inca system was so rigid that there was never any question about people knowing their exact place in it. Education was only for young nobles, who would one day lead armies or govern an alloted number of people. Although these young men usually came from the Inca royalty, sons of conquered rulers were often allowed these privileges, too.

Noble status was indicated by the clothes and jewelry a man wore. Commoners dressed simply, but the nobles and members of the royal family wore rich fabrics, bright feathers, and ornaments of gold and precious stones. The emperor himself wore the finest vicuña wool, which was thrown away at the end of each day.

Perhaps the most important sign of rank was the earplug, a gaudy kind of earring worn by men. The Inca were very proud of their earrings and considered them things of great beauty. The first Spaniards to see them were so impressed by them that they named the Inca *orejones,* which means "big ears."

The use of the earplug was the high point in a young Inca nobleman's life. After his schooling, which included wrestling, boxing, and long-distance marching, he knelt before the emperor and had his ears pierced by a gold dagger. He was not supposed to cry out at the pain, and when he rose he was considered a grown man. Gradually, the holes in his ears were made big enough to carry the earplugs. Some were enormous, and quite heavy. After being worn for a few years they brought a nobleman's ear lobes nearly to his shoulders.

The emperor to whom the young nobleman bowed was not only head of the Inca government, but of the army and priesthood as well. He was considered the sun god's divine son. To keep the bloodline pure, the emperor usually married his own sister.

Under a succession of emperors, and the class system they enforced, the Inca built great monuments. Their main fortress, which protected Cuzco in the southern Andes, was built out of rock and

A bold eye dominates this detail (at right) from an abstract design made of feathers. After 900 years, the feathers, taken from gaudy birds, remain bright.

136

Golden earplugs, inlaid with shell and turquoise, were worn 1,700 years ago by a Mochica nobleman.

Llama and wealthy citizen with outsize earplugs and headdress decorate clay vessel made by Inca potter.

defended by a thick wall 1,600 feet long. The way the Inca shaped and fitted stone is remarkable by any standard. They did not use metal tools or cement, yet many of their buildings are standing today. Machu Picchu, another stronghold, has more than a hundred stairways, some with as many as 150 steps. It is built on a series of levels on a mountain ridge 8,000 feet above sea level, and is so well designed that it seems a part of the mountains.

Among other things which the Inca took over from their predecessors was the art of working precious metals, especially gold. And it was this art, produced on a mass scale, which attracted the Spaniards who were eventually to conquer them. Word of the Inca gold treasure reached Francisco Pizarro and his company of less than two hundred soldiers in 1532.

Pizarro learned that Atahualpa, the Inca emperor, was encamped in the northern highlands, and led his men directly there. When Atahualpa came to meet him, Pizarro simply had him seized. The Inca nobles were so dependent on orders from above that they were helpless in the face of this bold move. Atahualpa offered Pizarro a room full of gold and silver for his freedom. Under his direction, the efficient Inca organization went to work. In a short while they gathered the ransom, a sum estimated at more than $8,000,000. But Pizarro did not keep his part of the bargain. The emperor was killed, and the Spaniards rode into Cuzco as conquerors.

The Inca noblemen were swiftly killed or driven into hiding, and with their departure the world of the Inca passed away. With its disappearance, and that of the Aztec empire to the north, little was left of one of the greatest cultural triumphs in the New World.

Yet, just as in Mexico, much of the past survives in the face of the Spanish civilization. More than 3,000,000 Andean Indians still speak the Quechua language of the ancient Inca. These people and other millions like them in South America can be proud of their heritage.

This display of Peruvian items shows plumed crown, earplugs, epaulettes, necklace, and 17-inch collar. On the right are fine examples of Mochica headdress.

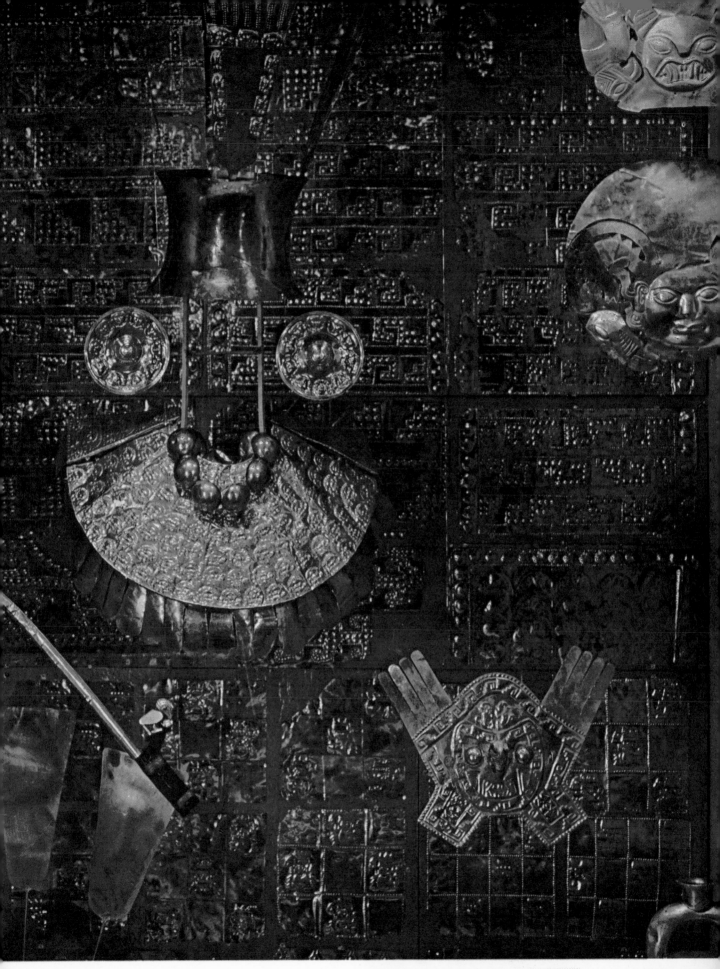

TODAY'S STONE AGE MEN

"It is clear," anthropologist Carleton S. Coon once said, "that all parts of the world, all of the members of the human family have not participated equally in the events that have marked the main line of human progress. . . . There are still marginal regions . . . where simple Stone Age hunters are suddenly confronted by strangers carrying rifles, where Neolithic garden-cultivators are trading their stone axes for steel ones and their pottery water jugs for discarded oil tins."

Many people have been passed by in man's progression from the first fire to the atom, from the wheel to space ships, from hieroglyphics to television. They still hunt, eat, and live together as men did in the Stone Ages. Some are close to those of the Old Stone Age, and use wooden spears tipped with stone points as their weapons. They have not yet discovered the bow and arrow, which appeared in the Middle Stone Age. Others live as did people of the New Stone Age, or the early Sumerians at the dawn of civilization.

For whatever reasons these people—most of them in remote places—were bypassed, they are

An Australian Aborigine aims a stone-tipped spear. His weapon is similar to devices used by Stone Age men in much the same way more than 10,000 years ago.

today important subjects of study for scholars. Their ways of life help us reconstruct the past. Along with the actual relics which have survived —paintings, sculpture, tools, and weapons—they come closest to giving us actual examples of how life may have gone on in man's earliest days.

The most numerous of modern people who live by Old Stone Age standards are the more than 70,000 Aborigines of Australia. Scholars do not know where they came from, or who their ancestors were. One theory is that they may be descended from an ancient people who came to Australia from the Asian mainland during a glacial period. The ocean levels were lower then and the water gaps shorter than they now are. Later, when the glaciers melted and the waters rose over the land causeways, these prehistoric travelers would have been isolated.

One reason the Aborigines may have continued in ways so nearly like the Old Stone Age peoples is the nature of Australia. In the hot, dry interior of this island continent few plants or animals could be domesticated. Thus, agriculture, the first requirement for civilization, was not developed.

Except for one major difference, the Aborigines of Australia are almost identical with the men and women who survived the glacial periods in Europe. Like Old Stone Age man, the Aborigine lives off the land with crude tools and weapons. But Old Stone Age man, living in rock shelters and caves, had to keep warm by newly discovered fire or the furs of animals. The Australian Aborigine, on the other hand, lives in a very hot climate, and for the most part wears no clothing. He sleeps in the open or builds temporary lean-tos of grass, bark, or leaves for protection against the tropical Australian climate.

Most of the Aborigine's life is spent hunting for food. To the men this is a search for kangaroos, lizards, alligators, and fish. The search is often long, and not always successful. Their stone-tipped spears are accurate weapons in their hands, but animals are not always available. To the women, the hunt is for wild figs, berries, grass seed, small reptiles, wood grubs, snails, water lilies, and wild honey. They look for these in the forests while the men are away, and always manage to find something edible.

Successful hunter holds two lizards he has caught. A twirling stick will start the fire to broil them.

To settle a feud, a killer stands ready to dodge spears thrown at him by members of dead man's clan.

141

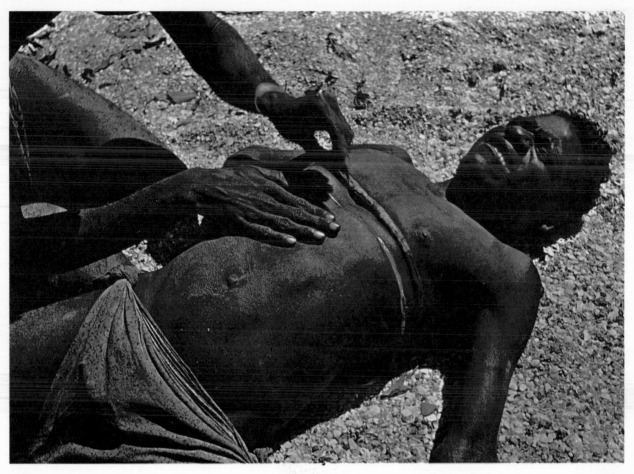

Decorative slash is cut on chest of Aborigine youth. This is part of the boy's initiation into manhood.

Painting on the bark of a eucalyptus tree depicts a women's dance, perhaps to encourage hunting success.

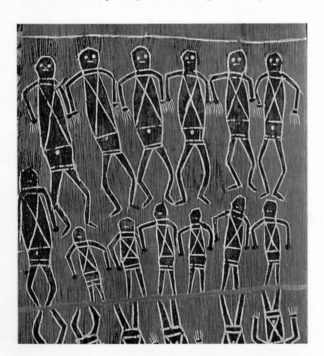

What the spear is to the hunter, the wooden bowl is to the Aborigine woman. It is her most important possession. In it she carries the fruits of her search in the forest, a child, or her possessions when the tribe moves to a new campsite. Like Old Stone Age utensils, it is made by using stone flakes to chop it from the hollow trunk of a tree.

Despite the extreme poverty of their existence the Aborigines have a religion of rich variety, and they use a language rich in meanings. "The absence of clothes and complicated economic systems does not imply an absence of thought," an anthropologist has said of primitive peoples. He could have been talking about the Aborigine, whose life is a partnership between himself and nature. He believes that if man does his part the spirits that control the natural world will work with him.

The Aborigine's part is carried out in worship and rituals designed to reach the powers in the spirit world. This unseen world, according to the Aborigine, is where all living creatures came from and where they will all return. As cave boys in the

Dancers celebrate tribal allegiance to their totemic ally, the wallaby, whose distinctive hop they imitate.

was the dog, and their most important social unit was the family.

As with the Aborigines, the origins of the Caribou Eskimos are unknown. They probably crossed to Canada when the Bering Strait was a land bridge between Siberia and Alaska. But how they got to the tundra—the treeless plains of the Arctic—is a mystery. Once there, however, they adapted to it, and unlike other Eskimos of Alaska, Canada, and Greenland, did not come face to face with civilization.

The Caribou Eskimos were almost completely isolated from the rest of mankind until 1949. Until then, their lives, with some important exceptions, were like those of Middle Stone Age men in Europe 10,000 years ago. The ancient Europeans found nuts, fruits, seeds, and wild grain. On the bleak tundra there are no edible plants except berries. Where Middle Stone Age men hunted

Weapons of the Caribou Eskimos for killing fish and caribou are similar to those used by Stone Age men.

Caribou Eskimo couple (right) are modern examples of people living like those of the Middle Stone Age.

Old Stone Age did, young Aborigines go through "rites of passage" before they can take part in grown-up activities. In "rites of intensification" the men act out the deeds of past heroes. This keeps traditions alive and helps to unify the clan.

In every part of his religious and social life, the Aborigine holds firmly to the idea of totemism. This is the belief that every person or group is the guardian of certain symbols and is allied with certain animals or plants. The totemic animal or plant is more than a mascot. It is believed to share the human's feelings. The totemic system can get quite complicated. A man may be allied not only with his own totem but to his family's and clan's as well. Under this system an Aborigine never feels alone.

Until very recently, the Caribou Eskimos lived on the northwestern shore of Hudson Bay in northern Canada. They grew no crops, but hunted and fished. Their spears, fish hooks, bows and arrows were of antlers, bone, and wood. They traveled in one-man kayaks; their only domesticated animal

deer, the Caribou Eskimos chased traveling herds of caribou, which provided them with food, clothing, tools, and weapons.

Like Middle Stone Age man, the Caribou Eskimo's life revolved around the family unit. Several families formed a camp, but this grouping was as temporary as the location of the camp itself. There were no tribal chiefs, but the camp's wisest hunter was treated as a headman. The shaman, or magic healer, was sometimes a leader because of his power to cast evil spells. Yet even this power was limited because the Caribou Eskimo's religion seldom influenced day-to-day life. Their god, named Pinga, lives in the sky. He guards the souls of men and beasts, and after death makes them live again in other bodies.

Since the caribou meant the difference between life and death, most of the Caribou Eskimo customs revolved around the hunt. Certain practices

An Eskimo elder repairs his kayak after an accident.

were forbidden lest they keep the caribou herds away from the hunters. None of the Caribou Eskimos owned land, and they considered their possessions less important than the good will of neighbors who worked with them in the hunt. The severest punishment was ostracism—being ignored by the members of the camp. This was usually prescribed for offenses like murder.

Labor among the Caribou Eskimos also followed the Middle Stone Age pattern. The men hunted, fished, and made the tools and weapons. The women pitched the caribou-skin tents, tended the fires, collected berries, cooked, sewed, gathered wood, and prepared skins and meat for drying. The separation of these duties was not always observed. Sometimes women were permitted to hunt, while the men sewed or cooked.

Marriages were arranged by parents for their children at an early age. The father of a daughter often received a gift of a kayak or a sled when such agreements were reached. The Caribou Eskimos were not limited to one wife, and some men had many. No matter how many wives a man had, the children received great care and love. This may have been because the birth rate was low and deaths among children high. A Caribou Eskimo child usually got what he wanted, and when he

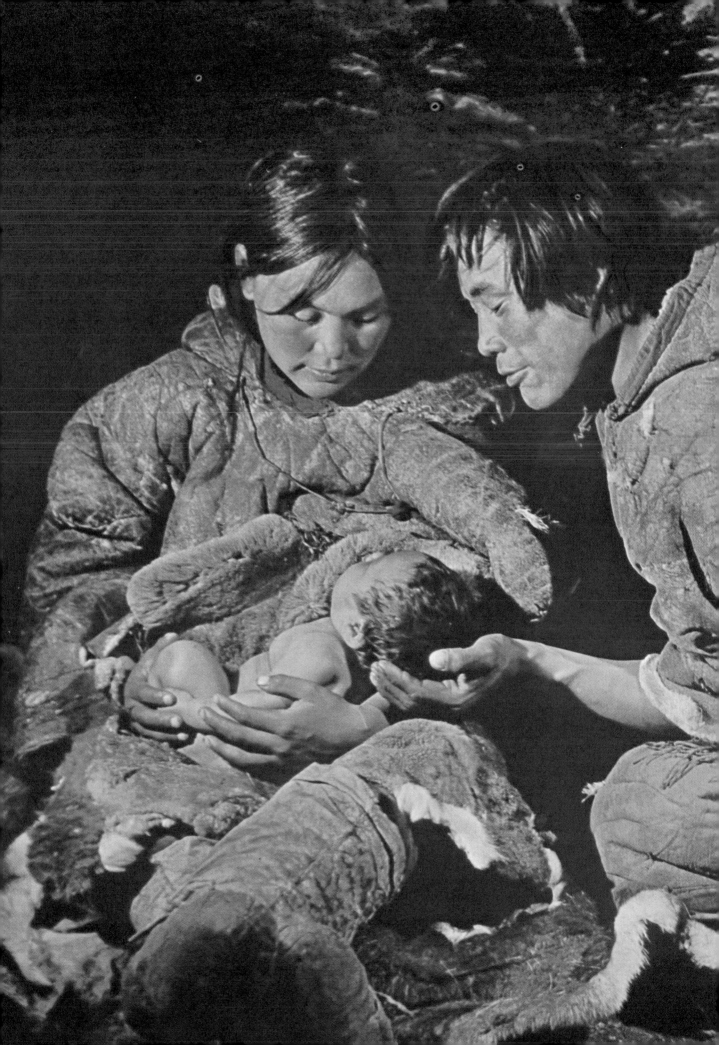

Caribou Eskimo parents care for their new son in the family tent. Babies are treasured by these people, and pampered more than children elsewhere.

cried all family activity stopped until he was made happy again. Children were never punished.

This kind of life survived for thousands of years under the most difficult of natural conditions. Its changes were few as long as the caribou herds appeared out of the south. Starting about a hundred years ago, the caribou herds grew smaller, and in some tragic seasons did not appear at all. The magic of the shaman was helpless as hunters returned with little or nothing to show for a day's effort. The answer lay not in magic but in the actions of modern men. The forests in which the caribou lived were being cut down and cleared. Hunters with guns instead of spears were killing caribou by the hundreds. In the absence of caribou, many Eskimos died, and life became grim for the living. "No caribou means no dogs, they die of starvation," an Arctic historian wrote. "It means

no food, no new clothing. It means hungry people that catch any germ that comes along."

In 1957, the Canadian government decided to resettle the Caribou Eskimos where they could receive supervised care. By that time, these primitive people had had a few years of contact with the white man. With it came diseases they had never known before, and the death rate went up. By the time the Eskimos were moved, their numbers had been reduced from several thousand to less than one thousand.

The impact of modern life has been hard on a people who survived under the standards of their ancient life. A few of them still hunt caribou, but there are not enough to go around. The Caribou Eskimos have in just a few years crossed many centuries. They have left behind the times when their young men had songs of their own, and used words like these to proclaim their skill:

I have been hunting caribou
And I killed them all:
Three of them, down by the lake.

Eskimo woman pegs wet caribou skins to dry in the sun. In autumn, camp rounds are covered with drying skins.

CHAPTER 15

TODAY'S TRIBAL MEN

In dozens of remote areas around the world today live a number of people—each group distinctive—who have one important thing in common. They still live as if this were the New Stone Age, that period in man's prehistory when he discovered farming, and just before he created the complicated system we call civilization. Some, like the Camayura Indians of Brazil and the Ainus in northern Japan, do not farm as extensively as did men of the New Stone Age. They cultivate meager gardens. Some, like certain New Guinea tribes, plant in one place until the soil is exhausted and then move on. Still others have advanced to irrigation systems and metal tools.

Among those who till the soil and herd their sheep in ways that existed before cities and states were established are the 30,000 Berbers who live on the southern slopes of the Atlas Mountains in Morocco. The center of their existence is a small river called the Dadès which forms a fertile valley north of the Sahara Desert. Its waters supply the irrigation ditches which the Berbers have dug to feed their fields of wheat and barley. Berber houses are made of pressed mud. Isolated in their rugged mountains, the Berbers did not have their ways changed by conquerors. Nor have they changed much today despite exposure to the modern world.

Scholars still do not know a great deal about the Berbers. The name itself is thought by some to come from the Greek word for "barbarian." They are probably descendants of the first known white settlers of North Africa, who started to arrive from the Middle East about 7000 B.C. There are many different Berber groups in Africa, with wide variations in appearance, who all speak different dialects of the Berber language.

It is likely that these differences came about over the years as small groups became isolated on mountains or near desert oases. The Berbers in the High Atlas Mountains are one of these distinctive groups. They are divided into two tribes, the Aït Hadiddou and the Aït Morrhad, that is, "the people of" Hadiddou and Morrhad. The tribes go their separate ways except when they join for defense against a common enemy.

The lives they lead, however, are identical, and follow a seasonal pattern year in and year out. The Dadès valley is fifteen miles long and only three miles wide. It holds just enough arable land to grow subsistence crops. The average family has two and a half acres. Each spring, as the rains begin, the Berbers start to work their fields. When the crops are planted, the flocks of goats, sheep, and a few cattle are led to the tribal pasturage

Berber girl holds the knife she uses to cut brush for fuel. She is wearing eye shadow made of grease and antimony, which Berber women think medicinal.

Tattooed young girl carries her baby brother in the fold of a blanket. They are of the Hadiddou tribe.

beyond the valley. The shepherds live there throughout the summer in tents made of goats' hair, returning to the valley in time to bring the harvest in. Late in September they travel fifty miles to a regional fair. There they buy and sell, dance, hold religious festivals, and perform marriages. Because of the way the work falls, autumn is the best time of year to marry. In winter little is done except for meetings of tribal councils, usually held in February. Soon after that, the spring rains begin, and the fields are made ready.

During these unchanging years the Berbers developed a community life which still suits them well. Fields and livestock are privately owned. Granaries and grazing land are communal property. Everyone is responsible for the protection of the granaries and the maintenance of the irrigation ditches. A village consists of the *ighs,* a group of related families. Several villages make up a clan, several clans a tribe.

In the winter tribal councils, the men vote for officers and judges. Each village elects a *mokallif,* or mayor, to serve for one year. Each tribe elects an *amrhar,* or chieftain, also for a one-year period. So that the various clans may have one of their own serve as village *amrhar,* he is not allowed to succeed himself in office. Judges are elected for three-year terms. There are seven of them, and they form a *jemaa n'lorf,* or court of customary law.

All civil and criminal cases are tried before this court. The goal of the judges is a decision which will be satisfactory to all parties. They usually succeed. When they do not, or when tempers are aroused, the judges simply adjourn the case. Sometimes an adjournment may last twenty years.

No records are kept of court cases because the Dadès Berbers, like other Berbers, have no written language. Their history is passed on from the old to the young by stories and traditions. Neither do they have any art forms beyond tribal songs and the simple tribal patterns they weave into their cloth or bake into their pottery. Although their religion is Islam, introduced by the Arabs, the Berbers also worship nature in special rituals.

The resources that are owned in common are the responsibility of the Berber men. They take turns guarding the granaries against desert nomads. On a strict schedule they irrigate the fields and maintain the *targa* through which the water flows from the Dadès to each plot of land. Individually, the Berber man has, besides farming and herding, the job of building and repairing his home, which is easily damaged by rain.

In general, outside of working the rocky ground, the Berber men's work is lighter than that of the women. From the age of eight, when Berber women are considered old enough to carry stacks of brush, they are expected to work hard. In the summer, when the men are with the herds, the women must cultivate the farms. They also spin and weave, cook and bake, milk the livestock and mill the grain. The most difficult work is the gathering of brush for winter fires. This is done late into the fall. By then the nearby crops of grass

Court of Custom of the Aït Hadiddou hears a witness testify. The elected judges follow ancient lore and try to reach decisions satisfactory to all parties.

Saharan Negro woman (above) spins yarn in primitive fashion. Below, Berber tribesmen build a mud house.

are gone, and the women have to trot as far as ten miles with their heavy loads.

Berber women are kept from doing many things by law and custom. It is considered "shameful" for one of them to ride a mule or donkey. They may buy, sell, or trade, but only a man can complete the transaction. If a widow inherits property, one of her husband's male relatives is named by the court to guard it. She may not sell it without his permission. When she does, he keeps one third of the land so that it may stay in the husband's side of the family.

The Aït Hadiddou allow women to take part in the festivities at the annual fall market. Among other things, that is where young women are sought out for marriage. It is also where the marriages themselves, usually of many couples at a time, take place. On marrying, a Berber woman does not take her husband's name, but keeps her father's. Berber men are allowed more than one wife, but a Berber woman may divorce her husband simply by moving out of his house.

Many efforts have been made to introduce modern ways to the Berbers of the Dadès valley, but they have not made much headway. When the French controlled Morocco, they tried to raise the Berber standard of living. Since Morocco won its independence in 1956, the Moroccan government has continued the French program. It has built schools and has tried to encourage the Berbers to send their children to them instead of to the mountains as herdsmen. But the Berbers' survival depends on the flocks and they do not see how they can spare their sons, least of all during the pasturing period.

The Moroccan government has responded to this with a plan for a local storehouse in which to keep fodder. Thus the herds would be fed, and the boys would be schooled. But the cost of fodder and of transporting it to the remote valley is very high. A paved road is being built to reduce these costs, but it is far from completed. In addition, new pastures are being developed in the dry area near the Dadès valley itself. This would help, too, but drilling water holes and paving irrigation ditches to save waste is also very costly.

The key to the problem is for the Berbers to settle into communities that are larger and more

Hadiddou women dogtrot across barren slopes with their loads of brush. The coarse grass is their only fuel.

permanent than their present small villages. So far little has been done about this. In recent years a few hopeful signs have been seen. In May, 1960, Morocco held its first local elections. Communes were set up, each with its own budget, to manage local affairs. Under a system of regional officers, the communes are linked to a governor at Ksar es Souk. This has given the villagers a sense of having a voice in their own affairs.

No sweeping changes have resulted, but a number of tribesmen seem eager to discuss ways to improve their lot. Some have even offered suggestions. The Berber population has been increasing at a rapid pace. The need to feed and clothe more people may be a greater pressure for change than that exerted by the Moroccan government.

Changes have been rare in the Berber way of life—a matter which does not seem to concern the tribesmen. When they are asked why certain things are done in certain ways, they usually shrug their shoulders. *"Aya d'asrif,"* they say. "It is the custom."

CHAPTER 16

THE OLD WAYS GO ON

The kingdom of Nepal lies in the Himalaya Mountains between India and Tibet on a narrow strip of land some five hundred miles long. Here, on mountain slopes and river valleys, millions of people have for centuries farmed land, herded sheep, and built cities. Three of these cities, each more than a thousand years old, lie in Nepal's Kathmandu Valley. They are Patan, Bhatgaon, and Kathmandu, the capital of Nepal. In them survives a form of civilization which in many ways resembles those of Sumer and Egypt at the dawn of history.

The Kathmandu Valley is an extremely difficult place to reach. To the north rise great mountain peaks, including Mount Everest, the highest in the world. To the south are tiger-infested jungles and rugged hills covered with densely packed elephant grass which grows fifteen feet high. Access to the valley is so difficult that for most of its history the only goods to get in and out of Kathmandu had to be carried on the backs of porters.

Despite such natural defenses, however, Nepal has often been conquered by strong invaders. A Negroid people, perhaps the original settlers of India, were probably the first to make their way through the southern barrier. They were followed by Mongolian peoples, driven north by Indo-Aryans who were expanding in northern India. Between 1000 and 700 B.C., the Indo-Aryans themselves entered Nepal. In the seventh century A.D. an invasion force from Tibet overran Nepal on its way to India. In 1769, Gurkha warriors, driven out of India by Moslem invaders, took over Nepal.

From all these people the civilization of Kathmandu Valley learned something new and adapted it for its own use. It was never absorbed by any of its invaders, but instead absorbed from them. The people mainly responsible for shaping the Kathmandu civilization are called the Newars. We do not know exactly when they arrived or where they came from. But they were established in the Kathmandu Valley by 563 B.C., when Gautama Buddha, the founder of Buddhism, was born in what is now southwestern Nepal.

The Newars are typical of the mixture of races in Nepal, especially in the Kathmandu Valley. In the northern part of the country, peoples like the Tamang and the Sherpa are short and yellow-skinned. Their religion is Buddhist and they speak a dialect influenced by Tibet and Burma. In the south, the Nepalese are tall and dark-skinned, practice Hinduism, and speak an Indo-Aryan dialect. The Newars are between the two in height and color. They speak Newari, which is a Tibeto-Burmese language, but they write in Sanskrit, which is Indo-Aryan. And they are both Hindu and Buddhist.

Bhairab, an incarnation of the Hindu god Siva, receives an offering. He is one of hundreds of Nepalese gods.

The Newars were great organizers and craftsmen. They built a widespread network of irrigation ditches to bring water to the farms in the valley. These are still used today for the raising of rice, the main food of Nepal. The Newars cut terraces into the sides of the hills, and planted fields there which were watered by the monsoon rains. Their wood carvers fashioned Hindu and Buddhist gods to be placed in the wood, stone, and brass temples designed by their architects. They used bricks for private houses which were built several stories high. And they built the three cities in the Kathmandu Valley which carry on today in much the same way they did when the Newars created them.

Kathmandu Valley contains 209 square miles of fertile land and more than 400,000 people. Most of them are farmers who work the land in family units made up of relatives from the father's side. Each day members of the family tend their tiny plot, which is often as small as a tenth of an acre and is usually rented from a large landowner. Others remain home to work at a traditional trade or craft such as pottery making. Many farm families live in thatch-roofed huts in villages near the rice fields. Others live in one of the three cities

A Newar woman with sleeping baby on her back plucks shoots. In Kathmandu, men plow while women plant.

which are all within walking distance of most of the rice fields.

A complicated caste system, based on family trades and crafts, separates one Nepalese group from another. But the Nepalese are not very rigid about it, and people sometimes move from one social class to another. The Nepalese also worship a wide variety of gods. Yet even though both the Buddhist and Hindu faiths exist, the people are practically united in worship. Some gods are respected by both faiths.

The shrines and temples of the gods are prominent in the three cities of the Kathmandu Valley. According to legend, the Indian emperor Asoka founded Patan in 250 B.C. He built five Buddhist shrines, four at each point of the compass and one in the center, thus giving the city the shape of the Buddhist Wheel of the Law. Bhatgaon, says the legend, was built in the hourglass shape of the drum of the Hindu god Mahadeva. Kathmandu took the form of the sword of the goddess Devi. As more temples and shrines were built, the cities grew up around them.

More than 2,500 shrines exist in the Kathmandu Valley, but only a few of them are purely Hindu or purely Buddhist. Hinduism arrived first in the valley. It was a religion based on the worship of many gods, but with one eternal spirit called Brahma. Hinduism also set up rigid racial and class lines, the basis of the caste system. Buddha's teachings were started in part to reform the caste system. Over the years most of the people of Kathmandu became Buddhists. But Buddhism was strongly influenced by Hinduism, and the two religions have continued side by side and strangely intermixed.

The ruler of Nepal is a Hindu, but when he was crowned in 1956, giant Buddhas were brought from the temples and given a place of honor in the coronation parade.

King Mahendra Bir Bikram considers this quite proper in the medieval country he rules, especially since he is eager to keep the people united to attain some measure of progress. King Mahendra succeeded his father as "King of Kings, Five Times Godly, Valorous Warrior and Divine Emperor." The royal line—the Shah dynasty—goes back to 1769, when the Gurkhas united Nepal.

Tamang girls wear holiday silks and traditional jewelry on visit to Kathmandu city from their country village.

Until very recently the Shah kings were not very strong rulers. For many years they were controlled by an aristocratic family called Rana. The Ranas kept Nepal all but hidden from the rest of the world. In 1950, King Tribhuvana overthrew the Ranas and opened the country to visitors from abroad.

King Tribhuvana died in 1955, but his son Mahendra did not become king officially until 10:43 A.M. on May 2, 1956. That was the precise moment chosen by the royal astrologers for the crown to be placed on his head.

The people of Nepal worship their king in much the same way that the ancient Egyptians worshiped the pharaoh—as a god-king. He is considered a representative on earth of the Hindu god Vishnu. When their king appears in public, the Nepalese clasp their hands in *namaskara,* the sign of reverence.

Under King Mahendra, Nepal is trying to catch up with the modern world. But the problems are enormous. Outside the Kathmandu Valley, the nation consists of thousands of scattered, primitive settlements. Many are overpopulated, and most of the people do not have enough to eat. Because of this separation, the 9,000,000 Nepalese do not have a tradition as a nation, but live as a group of tribal societies with very little in common.

Even if there were unity, the problems would be difficult. Rails and paved roads are rare in the mountainous land. It takes three weeks to travel three hundred miles from the Kathmandu Valley to the end of the kingdom. Only about ten percent of the soil can be cultivated. This amounts to about 6,500 square miles, not enough to feed the growing population. In trying to produce more, the Nepalese have terraced land as high as 10,000 feet above sea level. Some great landlords own as much as a million acres which they rent out in tiny plots

Milk is heated on kitchen hearth in Kathmandu home.

to Nepalese farmers. At best, these plots are barely enough to sustain a man's family.

Along the southern border of Nepal, where about three million people live, floods are a constant danger. In some parts of the country slavery still exists. The literacy rate is very low. Less than ten percent of the people can read and write. Most trade is carried on by bartering. And many of the ancient customs are still alive. Girls are sometimes "married" to trees before a regular marriage, for example. This is done so that they will not become widows if their human husbands die before they do.

Yet changes are taking place gradually, especially in the Kathmandu Valley. The old structure of family life is weakening. Where once families produced nearly everything its members needed,

Young boy (below) shapes clay pot on potter's wheel.

Tutor (below) teaches children Nepali and English.

Bathing in holy waters, devout Hindus worship at Pashupatinath, the shrine of the Lord of Beasts, on the Begmati River outside the city of Kathmandu. The river is revered by the Hindus as a source of the sacred Ganges.

they have now broken into smaller units. More people are buying in shops the things they used to make at home. Goods from outside the country are entering the cities and crowding out the goods of the local craftsmen. Many of the forms of group worship and celebrations are dying, too. People now seek such newly-imported pleasures as going to the movies.

Nepal joined the United Nations in 1956, and King Mahendra visited the United States with his queen, Ratna Devi, in 1960. These signs of the country's moves toward the outside world are matched by those which encourage outsiders to enter Nepal. Tourists may now visit the Kathmandu Valley without special permission, but they must have government approval to travel to other parts of the country. Foreign technicians have supervised many changes. American engineers are building roads and airstrips. Russians are building a cigarette factory and hydroelectric plant, while the Chinese are working on cement and paper factories.

Nepalese politicians have slowed down some of these advances by endless bickering. Some have been critical of the locations chosen for United States aid projects. While the government debates where a footbridge should be built, American steel

Classic Buddha (below) is attended by sacred monkeys.

King Mahendra and Queen Ratna Devi of Nepal ride an elephant through the heart of Kathmandu during the coronation parade. Nepalese guards lead procession.

lies rusting in the hills. The politicians are still not certain what course Nepal should take in the world at large. They hope to be neutral, and independent. They are so eager to be independent of India, for instance, that they keep the Nepalese clocks ten minutes ahead of Indian time.

The Nepalese may not be quite ready to handle the problems which face them. But in view of their history, the chances are good that they will be ready in the near future. The strange civilization of the Kathmandu Valley lived and became stronger as a result of the invasions and migrations which swept through it for thousands of years. Taking what each had to offer, and changing with the times, may have kept the Kathmandu civilization alive. The ancient ones it resembles most— the Sumerian and the Egyptian—crumbled because they resisted change.

The Nepalese seem to be following the advice of Milarepa, an eleventh-century Buddhist poet. "Hasten slowly and ye shall soon arrive," he wrote. It is likely that the Nepalese will absorb modern methods and make changes at their own pace, just as they have in the past.

Giant Buddhas brought from temples in and around Kathmandu await the coronation parade under fringed sunshades.

Indian women, wearing traditional saris, shovel coal from a freight car at a newly modernized steel plant.

EPILOGUE

FIVE THOUSAND YEARS LATER

In the twentieth century, less than 5,000 years after the dawn of civilization, man has developed tools which shrink distances, expand his life span, and open the door for even greater progress. Yet these tools are known and used by only about one third of the world's population—a billion people. The other two billion have been bypassed by most of modern technology. And of these, half still follow ways of life similar to those of the New Stone Age or even of more primitive times.

For people who still cling to the old ways, the sudden invasion of the new civilization has meant dislocation, upheaval, and strife. Some, like the Caribou Eskimos, have all but disappeared in the process. The Berbers on Morocco's Atlas Mountains remain stubborn in the face of change, and are fighting it. The people in the Kathmandu Valley may see the need for change, but are not eager to rush into it for fear they may lose their cultural heritage.

Lacking the gift of prophecy, no one can tell how the conflict between the old ways and the new will affect the peoples who are now engaged in it. The tribes, cities, and nations making the sudden leap from primitive to modern life are approaching it in different ways. Some, like China, are using any manufacturing method at hand—no matter how primitive—to bring themselves closer to the big industrial nations. Others, like India, are building a large industrial base by seeking assistance from the more advanced nations.

Whatever method is used, the changes are dramatic to watch. Devout North African Moslems on a pilgrimage to Mecca start their journey on camels and finish it on an airplane. Brazil has all but skipped the building of railroads and highways. It has gone directly from the horse and buggy to the airplane. In India, ten million oxcarts still carry most of the country's goods. In recent years many of these goods have been carried to factories which make railway cars, buses, and aircraft. In Africa, crude huts cluster near the gleaming white skyscrapers of booming cities.

As the centuries seem to run side by side in many parts of the world, it is not just industry which is affected. College students at the new university in the newly independent country of Nigeria spend most of their study hours on Western subjects. They want to become professional and scientific men and women on the American and European model. On the campus, some wear Western clothes, but most are still clothed in traditional West African garments. Nor can they quickly overlook the African traditions on which they were raised.

When the modern nations brought their forms of religion to primitive people, other important changes took place. As with education, the results have not always been clear cut, but often represent a mixture. In Latin America, the Roman Catholic Church wiped out the practice of human sacrifice from Mexico to Peru. But many of the old Indian gods have been incorporated into Catholicism, and are worshiped as saints. In Guatemala, descendants of the Maya burn incense on the steps of a four-hundred-year-old Catholic Church before they enter for Mass. They still believe the smoke carries their prayers upward to the almighty spirit.

In government, the nations which rose from the status of colonies have found that they cannot move overnight from old to new. In many of the new nations, the only effective forms of government were those found among the separate tribes. National leaders have had a difficult time convincing some of the tribal chiefs that they are now part of a larger unit. Where the colonial powers prepared the way for independence the transition was fairly smooth. The new leaders had been educated and had been given some experience in government. They understood some of the problems they would face and could help their people meet them. Where education had been discouraged, or where the changeover was sudden, chaos and civil war have often resulted.

As anthropologist Margaret Mead has said, mankind is "moving toward an interwoven, interconnected world." The speed of electronic communications and jet airplanes seems to be pushing all of mankind under one roof. The speech of a politician in Southeast Asia affects politicians in northwestern Europe. A radio broadcast in Cairo can start riots within the hour in Persian Gulf ports. A dance invented in the Caribbean may be banned in Indonesia. An American soft drink can start debates in the parliaments of half a dozen nations.

Yet it is this very interplay of one group with another which has had the greatest effect on the course of man's history since he left the caves. Almost every culture made a contribution to that of its neighbors, and thus to those which followed.

In Asia, the Shang established the patterns by which China has lived for centuries. In the Middle East, the Sumerians developed writing, the idea of money, and a decimal system. Egypt's ideas in government and science were spread by Phoenician traders and colonizers. The greatness of Greece was based on what the Minoans and Mycenaeans had started. The religious ideas of the ancient Hebrews became part of the traditions of Christianity and Islam. Many modern languages, including English, owe their form to the mixture of the Celts' language with the Latin of the Romans.

The record of the past is incomplete, and sometimes hard to read. Some civilizations have vanished, leaving only a few scraps of bones, a broken statue, some figures carved on stone. We often do not know who preceded or followed them. Others built on their immediate past, and changed into something else, which in turn was handed on to be changed again. What we are today is an accumulation of the cultures which managed to continue this process.

Man is not equipped to foretell the future. The measurements and projections of scientists are no more help than the shoulder-blade bones of the Shang. We can look back, though, and see where we have been, and how we got there. The story of man's past is not always a faithful guide for the future. All it really can do is help us understand the nature of the progress we have made so far. With that understanding we may be better prepared to face the future course of civilization.

Writing of the Greeks and Romans in words which can also apply to other early civilizations, the scholar Gilbert Highet has said:

"Those who are most easily depressed about the precarious future of Western civilization are usually people who do not know the full history of its past. . . . Progress has not been continuous throughout the last three thousand years of our history— nor the last three hundred; nor even the last thirty. . . .We, who stand lower than the Greeks and Romans in some things and higher in others, can and should look toward them constantly, in order to interpret our own destinies."

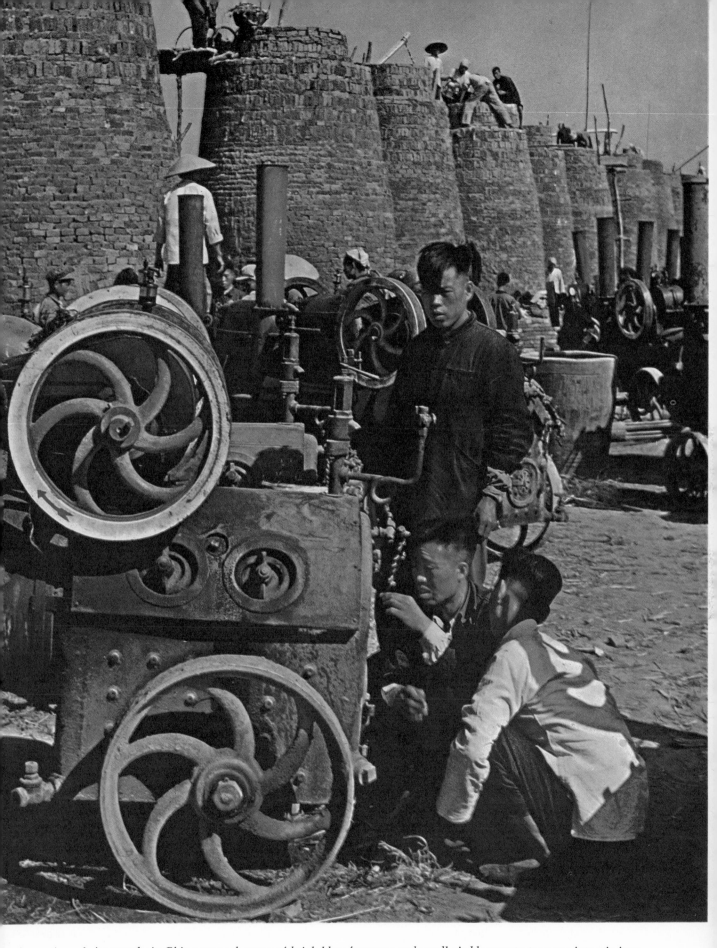

A crude ironworks in China uses a battery of brick blast furnaces and small air blowers to turn ore into pig iron.

Jet planes and oxcarts, centuries apart in the history of transportation, make a sharp contrast outside a new

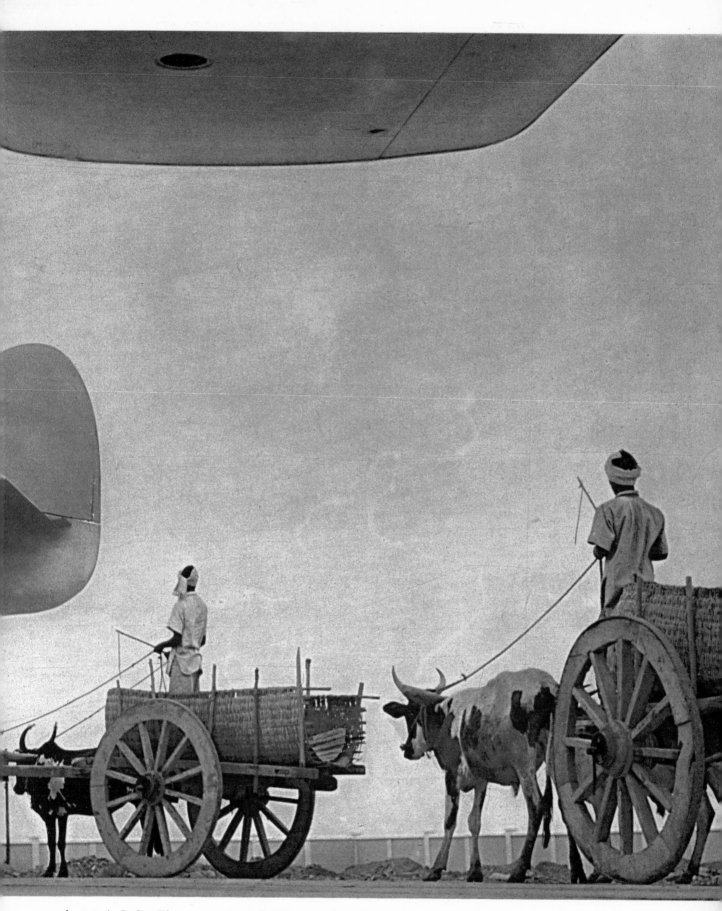

factory in India. The carts go back 5,000 years. The plant turns out cars, buses, and the latest airplanes.

THE TIMES OF MAN

Early Evolutionary and Cultural Periods

DATES	AMERICA	EUROPE	AFRICA-MIDDLE EAST	ASIA
70,000,000 First primate				
30,000,000 Anthropoid apes				
700,000 Ice ages begin			600,000 Zinjanthropus	500,000 Java man
500,000-100,000 Acheulian age			400,000 Chellean man	360,000 Peking man
250,000 Homo sapiens		250,000 Steinheim and Swanscombe men		
		150,000 Fontechevade man		
100,000-35,000 Mousterian age		100,000 Neanderthal man		
		75,000 Fourth ice age begins		
35,000-8000 Upper Paleolithic (Europe)		35,000 Combe Capelle man		
35,000-28,000 Lower Perigordian		28,000-14,000 Cro-Magnon man	23,000 Rhodesian man	
28,000-21,000 Aurignacian	20,000 Ancestors of American Indians cross Bering Strait from Asia			
21,000-18,000 Upper Perigordian		18,000 Fourth retreat of glaciers		
18,000-14,000 Solutrean		14,000-8000 Magdalenian man		
14,000-8000 Magdalenian				
8000-5000	8000 Human settlements extend to Strait of Magellan		8000 Neolithic revolution takes place in the Middle East	
			8000 Founding of Jericho	
5000-4000			4500 Farming starts in Egypt	
			4500-2900 Rise of civilization in Sumer	
4000-3000			3500-2500 First cities rise in Nile and Tigris-Euphrates valleys	3500-2500 First cities rise in Indus valley
			3100 Menes unites Egypt	
3000-2000		3000 Neolithic farming starts in Europe	2700 Old Kingdom begins in Egypt	2500 Farming begins on the North China plain
	2500 Farming under way in Middle and South America		2600-1200 Egyptian dominance in Syro-Palestine	2500 Start of Indus Valley civilization
			2500 Sumerian Royal Tombs built at Ur, Bronze Age begins	2500 Mastery of the horse in central Asia
			2360-2180 Semites establish Akkadian Empire	
			2160 Fall of Egyptian Old Kingdom	
			2100-2025 Ur-Nammu unites Sumer and Akkad. Period of Sumerian renaissance	
			2050 Start of the Middle Kingdom in Egypt	
2000-1000		2000-1400 Minoan civilization in Crete	2000 Abraham leaves Haran in northern Mesopotamia	2000 Height of Indus civilization at Harappa and Mohenjo-daro
		1900 Mycenaeans reach Greece from the north	1900 Hittites conquer north-central Anatolia	1700-1100 Shang civilization. Bronze Age begins in China
	1500 B.C.-300 A.D. Maya Pre-Classic age	1450-1150 Mycenaean maritime domination	1728-1686 Rise of Babylon. Hammurabi issues Law Code	
		1450-1400 Mycenaean rule in Knossos	1567 New Kingdom begins in Egypt	
		1400 Start of metallurgy in northern Europe. Bronze Age begins	1400 Hebrews invade the land of Canaan	
			1370 Akh-en-Aton tries to convert Egypt to monotheism. Hittites move into northern Syro-Palestine	